CW00958135

A COMPENDIUM OF PRACTICAL MUSIC
IN FIVE PARTS

CHRISTOPHER SIMPSON

A Compendium of

PRACTICAL MUSIC

IN FIVE PARTS

EDITED AND WITH AN INTRODUCTION BY

PHILLIP J. LORD

*Formerly Lecturer in Music
in the University of Sheffield*

*Reprinted from
the Second Edition of* 1667

BASIL BLACKWELL
OXFORD
1970

© *Basil Blackwell* 1970

631 12610 4

All rights reserved. No part of this publication may be reproduced, stored in any retrieval system, or transmitted in any form or by any means, electronic, mechanical, photocopying, recording or otherwise, without the prior permission of the Copyright owner.

Engraved and printed in Great Britain by Compton Printing Ltd., London and Aylesbury and bound by Kemp Hall Bindery, Oxford

CONTENTS

CONTENTS vii

PAGE

13. Of Music composed for Voices 75
14. Of Accommodating Notes to Words . . . 77
15. Of Music Designed for Instruments . . . 77

THE FIFTH PART: THE CONTRIVANCE OF CANON . . 80

1. Concerning Canon 80
2. Canon of Two Parts 81
3. Canon of Three Parts 83
4. Of Canon in Unison 84
5. Of Syncopated or Driving Canon . . . 85
6. Of Canon a Note Higher or Lower . . . 90
7. Of Canon Rising and Falling a Note . . . 91
8. Of Retrograde Canon or Canon Recte and Retro . 91
9. Of Double Descant 93
10. Of Canon to a Plainsong Proposed . . . 94
11. Of Catch or Round 96

APPENDIX: SHORT AND EASY AYRES DESIGNED FOR LEARNERS . 99

EDITOR'S PREFACE

THE second edition of the *Compendium* (1667) was the only complete copy of the book to be published during Simpson's lifetime and it has therefore been made the basis of this present edition. It is, however, possible that Simpson may have commenced work on the preparation of the third edition during the last two years of his life (1667–1669), although this edition was not published until 1678.

In one particular respect there is a major discrepancy between the texts of the second and third editions. This occurs on pages 63–66 and consists of an addition to the text of the second edition. A complete chapter entitled 'Concerning the Consecution of Perfects of the same kind and of other Disallowances in Composition' is added in the third edition. Simpson was responsible for the addition, and this chapter is included in an appendix to the second edition.

Apart from this important alteration, there are only a few minor differences between the second and third editions; in such cases as these the original second edition version is given but some sentences which appear for the first time in the third edition are included in the text of the present edition and remarked upon in footnotes. It is interesting to note that the first part of the *Compendium*, 'The Rudiments of Song,' is identical in the second and third editions, whereas in the other four parts of the book one major and several minor alterations are evident. In the fourth and subsequent editions it was 'The Rudiments of Song' which suffered at the hands of editors in attempts to bring the book into line with current musical notation; the other four parts of the book remained comparatively unaltered. The original manuscript of the *Compendium* is contained in the library of St. Michael's College, Tenbury, and is listed as MS.390, although its authenticity is open to question.

The following modifications have here been made to the original printed text:

1. The punctuation has been revised, numerous pairs of brackets enclosing phrases in parenthesis having been removed, and Simpson's use of capitals and italics curtailed. Omitted letters (e.g. engag'd, referr'd) have been replaced. Redundant apostrophes have been removed and certain antiquated abbreviations, such as 2d, 3d, modernized.

2. The few editorial additions to Simpson's text are enclosed in square brackets.

3. The spelling of certain words has been revised: e.g.—adjoyned, aire, applyed, etc.

4. Some words have been modernized: accompt account, alt alto, begun began, concernments concern, compt count, designment design, explicate explain, holden held, mathematick mathematical, mechanick mechanical, practick practical, rations ratios, shewed shown, stupendious stupendous.

5. Archaic words are replaced by their modern equivalents when they confuse the meaning of the text. Any such changes are mentioned in footnotes, as are also the original spellings of those musical forms mentioned by Simpson.

Footnotes have been given for one of the following reasons:

1. To show differences between the second and third editions.
2. To indicate any alterations to the original text.
3. To clarify obscurities.
4. To remark on points of special interest.
5. To supply cross references.
6. To give details of composers and theorists mentioned in the text.
7. To quote full titles of works mentioned in the text.

When clefs or key signatures have been altered in the musical examples, the originals are also given. Note values are unchanged. Simpson prefixes few time signatures, and only when he uses the time signature 3 have modern equivalents been given. Although the musical examples are barred regularly in the second edition, bar lines do not always occur frequently and in such cases dotted bar lines have been added. Accidentals have been revised, e.g. F ♮ instead of F♭, and those which are redundant have been removed. Dots which follow bar lines and represent the second of two tied notes have been modernized.

In the 'Appendix of Short and Easie Ayres Designed for Learners' Simpson uses the repeat signs ┤╞ and 𝄋 which have been modernized (see footnotes 19 and 20 on pp. 12 and 13). Occasionally the pause mark ⌢ is omitted in one part and present in the other. In such cases the missing pause has been supplied (see footnote 21 on p. 13). In view of the wide range of the parts in the six pieces 'For two Bass-Viols,' a variety of movable C clefs was used in the third edition. It has been impossible to indicate the original changes of clef, and the changes from 𝄞 to 𝄢 in the present edition do not correspond to changes from 𝄡 to 𝄢 in the original. Key signatures are re-stated after each change of clef in the third edition. In all the pieces the occasionally omitted bar lines and rests have been supplied, and unnecessary bar lines removed. Points of interest are mentioned in footnotes. Occasionally phrase or bowing marks occur and these have been retained in the present edition.

I should like to express my gratitude to all those who have helped in any way with the publication of this edition, but in particular I must acknowledge the support and encouragement I have received from Dr. E. D. Mackerness of Sheffield University and Charles Cudworth, Librarian of the Pendlebury Library, Cambridge. I must also thank the Sheffield University Research Fund for generous assistance.

P. J. Lord

Sheffield, 1969

INTRODUCTION

CHRISTOPHER SIMPSON'S LIFE AND WORKS

Very little is known about Simpson's life, although details have come to light regarding his immediate family. He was the eldest son of Christopher Simpson and his wife Dorothy Pearson, and was probably born during the first decade of the seventeenth century. The Harleian MS. 5800, folio 21 in the British Museum, which shows his coat of arms, traces Simpson's family back to his great-grandfather, 'Christopher Sympson, descended from that name and Familie originally in Nottinghamshire.' Many of the other members of the family mentioned are connected with places in Yorkshire in the district of Goathland, near Whitby, with the exception of Simpson's grandfather who is described as 'George Sympson of Richmond in Yorkshire.' The composer's father came from Westonby and his mother from Rostall, which is probably the local pronunciation of Rosedale. The composer himself is referred to as 'Christopher Sympson of Hunthouse in ye wapentake of Pickering in ye County of Yorke.'

His parents moved to Egton, near Goathland, after they married; their names appear in a *List of Roman Catholics in the County of York in 1604*.[1] Under the heading 'Egton' is written, 'Xpofer Sympson of Egton cordwayner,[2] Dorothie his wife,' and on the next page in a list of couples living together, still under Egton,

> Chrofer Simpson, Dorothie Pearson; . . . all thes lyve together as man & wife and suspected to be secretly marryed.

It is therefore likely that the composer was born at Egton and perhaps not before 1604, as the names of his parents are not included in a list of private baptisms in the same MS. under the heading, 'All these have had children baptised privately of late yeares.'

It is possible that Simpson spent his early years in this district of Yorkshire and that he may have been an apprentice in the family trade of shoemaking, but when his musical ability first began to show itself or how he acquired his knowledge of music is completely unknown. Fétis[3] remarks that '[il] paraît avoir été attaché dans sa jeunesse à quelque chapelle, peut- être même à celle du roi Charles Ier. . . .' The authority, if any, for this statement is not quoted and it is questionable, Simpson

[1] Edited by Edward Peacock, F.S.A., London, 1872, p. 97.
[2] = shoemaker. Edward Sympson, also a shoemaker and probably the composer's uncle, appears in this list.
[3] Francois J. Fétis, *Biographie Universelle des Musiciens*, 2nd ed., Paris, VIII (1875), 45.

being a Roman Catholic. If Simpson remained in this remote district until the civil war, he may have been an amateur musician and was perhaps self-taught.

In the dedication of the second edition of the *Compendium* to William Cavendish, 1st Duke of Newcastle, Simpson mentions that he served under the Duke during the Civil War. Most authorities give 1643 as the date of Simpson's enlistment and this may very well be correct. It is perhaps significant that Newcastle's army was stationed in the north at York (about thirty miles away from Simpson's native area) at this time, awaiting reinforcements.

Newcastle led many strenuous campaigns throughout 1643 and 1644 beginning with the attack on the West Riding (2nd April, 1643) and the occupation of Wakefield, Rotherham and Sheffield. Simpson may have been sent to Oxford with a large portion of Newcastle's forces as escort to the Queen, or been present at the defeat of the Fairfaxes at Adwalton Moor (30th June). No doubt the events of 1644, the march north in bad weather to oppose the Scots, the defeat at Selby, the retreat back to York and the siege of the city which followed—all these events would have affected his condition, both physically and mentally. Circumstances in early July, 1644, decided Newcastle to leave the country. Whether Simpson left the army then or continued in the struggle is unknown. If he went back to his home in the Goathland district it would be to a place where the Parliament forces were the masters and a Catholic Royalist not likely to be looked upon with much favour.

Evidence concerning the events of Simpson's life after the Civil War is to be found in the dedication of the second edition of his book, *The Division-Viol*,[4] to Sir John Bolles, Bart. The first edition was dedicated to Sir Robert Bolles, as Simpson reminded his son Sir John in the new dedication:

This Treatise, upon the first Publication, was Dedicated to your late Father, and not without good reason; for, all the Motives that could enter into a Dedication of that nature, did oblige me to it. First, as he was a most eminent Patron of Musick, and Musitians. Secondly, as he was not only a Lover of Musick, but also a great Performer in it. Thirdly, as the said Treatise had its Conception, Birth, and Accomplishment under His Roof, in your Minority. Lastly, as he was my peculiar Patron; affording me a cheerful Maintenance, when the Iniquity of the Times had reduced me (with many others in that common calamity) to a condition of needing it.

Simpson's life after the Civil War was one of privation until his meeting with Sir Robert Bolles, who was sympathetic towards Simpson's views, being a confirmed Royalist himself and a patron of

---

[4] Christopher Simpson, *The Division-Viol*, ed. by Nathalie Dolmetsch, a facsimile of the 2nd edition, London, 1955.

the arts.[5] It is not known how he came to meet Simpson; perhaps they met during the Civil War since Newcastle's forces were in Lincolnshire in July and August, 1643. Simpson lived with the Bolles family in the capacity of tutor at the Manor of Scampton in Lincolnshire. His pupils were Sir Robert's son, John, and a certain Sir John St. Barbe, to whom the 1665 edition of the *Compendium* was dedicated. John Bolles proved to be a talented musician. He visited Rome in 1661, probably accompanied by Simpson, who praises his abilities in the dedication to the second edition of *The Division-Viol* and prints verses written in his honour by a certain Italian, 'occasion'd by your rare Expressions on the Viol at a Musick-meeting.' Another pupil may have been William Marsh, who translated *The Division-Viol* into Latin for the second edition.[6] When Sir Robert Bolles died in August, 1663, he left a large fortune to his seven children. His will was witnessed by Simpson, to whom he bequeathed the sum of five pounds. John Bolles, the eldest surviving son, succeeded his father to the title, and inherited the manor and estate of Scampton. It may be that there was some doubt in Simpson's mind when his patron died as to whether he would be retained in the service of the Bolles family and perhaps with this in mind he bought Hunt House, near Pickering in Yorkshire. Otherwise it seems curious that a musician living in Lincolnshire should buy a farm in Yorkshire. Hunt House[7] lies at the foot of the Egton High Moor, Simpson's home country, in an area which had remained comparatively unaffected by the Reformation. It was therefore a very suitable retreat where Simpson might have lived quietly, if his services at Scampton were no longer required by his former pupil. But this was not to be; he was retained in service and settled the property of Hunt House on his nephew, also called Christopher Simpson.

Different authorities quote varying dates for the year of Simpson's death. He made his will on 5th May, 1669, and probate was granted to his executors, William Simpson (his nephew) and Francis Pearson (a cousin?) on 29th July of the same year. He therefore died at some time between these two dates. If we are to believe Anthony à Wood, Simpson died about May 29th of that year. On that date Wood wrote in his diary: 'Mr. Simpson the musitian, a composer, died this month

[5] Details of the life of the Bolles family are to be found in the Rev. Cayley Illingworth's *Topographical Account of the Parish of Scampton . . .*, London, 1808. Sir Robert Bolles was one of the Grand Jury for trying the Regicides at Hick's Hall in 1660.

[6] An ambiguous remark by Simpson in the dedication of the second edition of *The Division-Viol*, referring to the Latin translation of his book, might mean that Marsh was one of Simpson's pupils. '. . . yet one thing I must acquaint you with, which is, That our Division-Viol Sounds better now in Latin than it formerly did in English; the Gentleman that hath improv'd it is your kind Acquaintance, my ever honoured Friend (and Sometime Scholar in Musick) Mr. William Marsh, . . .'

[7] This house, which has a history dating back to 1296 in the *North Riding Records*, was to remain in the possession of the Simpson family well into the eighteenth century.

at Sir John or Sir William Bolls.'[8] But at some later date he added to this entry: 'Sure he was living after this,' and having secured confirmation of his suspicions, he added to the same entry later still the word 'True.' It is not known at which of the residences of Sir John Bolles Simpson's death occurred. A note by Wood found at the beginning of an Almanac for 1670 reads: 'Anno 1669, Mr. Christopher Sympson, a famous musitian died at Sir John Bool's hous; whether in Lyncolnshire or at London, I knowe not.'[9] Hawkins[10] says that Simpson 'dwelt some years in Turnstile, Holborn, and finished his life there,' but Burney[11] refers to Simpson's patron as Sir Robert Bolles of Leicester-place.

Simpson's will shows also that his financial state was not very secure in 1669, apart from the Hunt House property. Most of the money from his publications must have been spent in acquiring this house and farm. Various sums of money bequeathed to his relatives are charged to Hunt House and made the responsibility of his nephew Christopher Simpson. The will reads:

> And whereas I have by deed and fine passed settled Hunthouse and the farm thereunto belonging upon my nephew Christopher Simpson after my decease, reserving in my self the power to charge upon it what debts and legacies I shall think fit by will or otherwise, I do by this my present will charge upon it and bind my said nephew Christopher to the payment of these following debts and legacies in this my will expressed.

Various items, such as repayment of loans and gifts of money are 'for better security' charged to Hunt House in case the money either 'be not paid before my death' (repayment of loans) or 'be not otherwise secured' (bequests). Simpson left very little apart from a few rings, clothes and books. His music books he bequeathed to Sir John Bolles who was also one of the executors of the will. From the terms of the will it may be assumed that Simpson never married.

Simpson's reputation as a composer, performer and author stood high in his own day. During his lifetime, consort music for viols and violins was the main form of instrumental music, and his own compositions are chiefly for stringed instruments. Several contemporary writers refer to him, and he had many friends among the main composers of the day. Thomas Mace wrote of him:

> These last Ages have produc'd very many Able, and most Excellent Masters in Musick; Three only (of which) I will instance in, in This Particular; because they were so Voluminous, and very Eminent in Their Works, viz. Mr. William Lawes, Mr. John Jenkins, and Mr. Christopher Simpson.

---

[8] Andrew Clark, ed., *The Life and Times of Anthony Wood*, in *Oxford Historical Society*, **XXI** (1892), 162.   [9] *Ibid.*, p. 181.
[10] Sir John Hawkins, *A General History of the Science and Practice of Music . . .*, London, II (ed. of 1875), 708.   [11] Charles Burney, *A General History of Music*, London, III (1789), 422.

These Three Famous Men, although Two of Them be laid asleep, (or as we say, Dead;) yet by Their most singular and Rare Works, They Live; and may so easily be Distinguished, the one from the other, and as Exactly known, which is which, as if they were present in person, and should speak Words.[12]

One of Simpson's most influential friends was Sir Roger L'Estrange (1616–1704), an ardent Royalist who led a most adventurous life, and whose name, as one of the licencers of the press, appears in Simpson's books. Although an amateur, he was ranked as one of the greatest performers on the bass viol together with John Jenkins and Simpson. North describes him in his *Memoirs* as an expert violist.[13] We may believe L'Estrange's testimony when he speaks highly of Simpson in his letter of recommendation in *The Division-Viol*:

Briefly; As to the Command, and Mastery of the Viol, (in that point which is the Excellency of That Instrument) either for Hand, or Skill, I will take upon me to aver, that whoever has This Book by him, has one of the best Tutors in the world at his Elbow.

L'Estrange also speaks well of Simpson's moral character in a similar letter published in the *Compendium*; other contemporary accounts also make reference to his personal integrity. Thomas Salmon, the Rector of Mepsall, and Mathew Locke, the composer, made use (in their famous quarrel) of Simpson's moral reputation to confound each other. Locke in his *Observations* on Salmon's book wrote: 'He [Salmon] abuses Mr. Christopher Simpson (a Person whose memory is precious among good and knowing Men for his exemplary life and excellent skill)' to which Salmon countered, 'Simpson . . . whom indeed I greatly honour, for that double accomplishment of his exemplary life, as well as excellent skill; and know nothing more necessary than to commend the former to my Observer's imitation.' Simpson's moral standing was too high to suffer as a result of this controversy. John Jenkins was a true friend to Simpson as was also Mathew Locke, and their letters of commendation are given on page xlvii. Sir John Hawkins knew the *Compendium* and *The Division-Viol* very well and gives a lengthy account of both; Burney considered Simpson 'a musician extremely celebrated for his skill in the practice of his art, and abilities on his particular instrument.'

These judgements, for the most part refer to Simpson as author and performer. An assessment of his reputation as a composer is more difficult to make since many of his compositions are still in manuscript.

[12] Thomas Mace, *Musick's Monument*, London, 1676, p. 151.
[13] John Wilson, ed., *Roger North on Music*, London, 1959, p. 355.

The following manuscripts containing works by Simpson are in the British Museum:

(a) Add. MS. 18940–18944. Suites in 3 parts. 21 pieces for 3 viols with an added continuo part, consisting of 3 pavanes, 2 galliardes, 5 allemandes, 6 courantes and 5 airs. These are mentioned in Hughes-Hughes's *Catalogue of Manuscript Music in the British Museum*, III, 184.

(b) Add. MS. 31436, ff. 13–25, 39b–51, 65b–77, 91–96b. A set of 12 pieces named after the months of the year. This has been wrongly attributed to Hingeston. The entry in Hughes-Hughes, *ibid.*, p. 270, is incorrect.

(c) Add. MS. 31436, ff. 26b–38, 52b–64, 78b–90, 97–100b. A set of 4 groups of pieces, each containing a Fancy, an Air and a Galliard, and named after the seasons. They are in 3 parts with a partly-figured bass.

(d) Add. MS. 39555. This MS. is a tracing of a seventeenth-century lute manuscript and shows four lute pieces attributed to 'C S' (ff. 9b–10, 12b–13, 13b–14, 17b–18) and a set of two pieces, the second called 'A Sarabande' and attributed to 'Ch: Simpson' (f. 32b). The original MS. belonged to the Rookwoods of Coldham and the Gages of Hengrave; its present location is unknown.

The Bodleian Library is in possession of the following manuscripts of Simpson's compositions:

(e) MS. Mus. Sch. D 220. An Ayre and Corant; one part only, of two.

(f) MSS. Mus. Sch. E 431–6. Ayres and various other pieces for strings.

(g) MSS. Mus. Sch. E 447–9. Ayres and various other pieces for two treble viols and bass.

(h) MS. Mus. Sch. C 59–60. Pieces for two division viols and ground.

(i) MS. Mus. Sch. C 71. Divisions.

(j) MS. Mus. Sch. F 568–9. Four part lessons. (Incomplete.)

(k) MS. Mus. Sch. C 77. Pieces for two bass viols.

G. E. P. Arkwright's *Catalogue of Music in the Library of Christ Church, Oxford*, London, 1923, has three entries under C. Simpson. They are:

(l) 1021. Bass part of 26 pieces in suites.

(m) 1027. Treble part of 21 pieces.

(n) 1183. Two Grounds in C for instruments. Bass and Ground only.

The *Catalogue of Manuscripts in the Library of St. Michael's College, Tenbury*, compiled by Edmund H. Fellowes, Paris, 1934, has this entry:

(o) '296–299. Christopher Sympson's Fancies for strings upon the Four Seasons of the year. Three instrumental parts with basso continuo bound together in four books, with their original covers. In the composer's autograph.'

An article on Simpson in Grove's *Dictionary*, 5th ed. (1954), lists several of the above MSS. and in addition mentions:

(*p*) MS. No. 3193 in the Municipal Library of Hamburg.[14] Consorts of Parts for two Trebles and two Basses with figured bass. Contains 20 pieces.

(*q*) A manuscript (music) mentioned by Sir William Musgrave in *An Obituary of the Nobility, Gentry, etc.*, and dated 1666. Musgrave's work is included in *Collectanea Genealogica*, I, ed. Joseph Foster, London, 1887.

The Royal College of Music possesses a printed copy of *The Division-Viol* which contains manuscript additions of the seventeenth century including:

(*r*) Two divisions on a ground for viol in D by Simpson (ff. 10, 10b).

To this list Jeffrey Pulver makes the following additions:[15]

(*s*) A vocal piece, 'I saw fair Chloris walk alone.' This is contained in the *Musical Companion*, 1672, No. 49.

(*t*) A piece by Simpson contained in Playford's *Division-Viol*, 1685. This is also mentioned by Eitner.

(*u*) Eight short pieces contained in Playford's *Court Ayres*, 1655.

Murray Lefkowitz mentions pieces by Simpson included in:

(*v*) Part II, entitled *Musica Harmonia* from *A Musicall Banquet*, 1651, containing pieces by Charles Coleman, Richard Cooke and William Lawes as well as by Simpson. The only known copy of this work is to be found in the Bodleian Library.[16]

In addition, Simpson's two books both contain pieces written by himself. The 1665 edition of the *Compendium* contains 'Some Short and Easie Ayres Designed for Learners' as does the 1678 edition, but some of these pieces are not by Simpson. There are sixteen pages of 'Divisions for the practice of Learners' in the appendix to *The Division-Viol*.

Simpson's earliest theoretical writings are to be found in the annotations to Thomas Campion's short treatise, *A New Way of Making Fowre Parts in Counter-point*, 1613, which was included in the second edition of John Playford's *Brief Introduction to the Skill of Musick* in 1655 under the title of *The Art of Setting or Composing of Musick in Parts. . . .* Campion's treatise continued to be included in subsequent editions of Playford's book until 1683, when an essay by an unknown author

---

[14]Grove quotes Heidelberg, not Hamburg, probably misreading the abbreviation 'B. Hbg.' in Eitner's *Quellen-Lexicon*. See Jeffrey Pulver's article on Simpson in *The Musical News*, Feb. 12th, 1916. [15]Pulver, *op. cit.* [16]M. Lefkowitz, *William Lawes*, London, 1960, p. 34.

(possibly Playford himself), entitled *An Introduction to the Art of Discant*, replaced it, probably to bring the book up to date. This was eventually superseded in the 12th edition, 1694, by an article entitled, 'An Introduction to the Art of Descant or Composing Musick in Parts,' by Henry Purcell, who also revised the whole book. Playford, in his introduction to the edition of 1660, wrote:

> This Litle Book of Dr. Thomas Campion's, which (for the Excellency and Compendious Method it bears in the Rules of Descant or Composing Musick into Parts) hath found so General acceptance, that two Impressions of It have been bought up already; which doth encourage me once more to publish it to the World, and that with Additional Annotations thereon, by that Excellent and profound Master of Musick, Mr. Christopher Simpson. Those who desire to know more concerning Counterpoint, and the Rudiments of Composing Musick of 2, 3, 4, or more Parts and the use of Discords, I refer them to the First Part of the said Mr. Christ. Simpson's Book lately published Entituled The Division Violist; which Book may justly be counted the Master-piece of this Age, for the Excellent Rarities of Musick set forth therein.

Simpson wrote *The Division-Viol or, the Art of Playing Ex tempore upon a Ground. Divided into Two Parts* while at the home of Sir Robert Bolles, and it was published in 1659. The second edition, in three parts, appeared in 1667, not 1665 as originally intended. In this edition a Latin translation was added to the original text, as Simpson wrote in the preface, 'that it might be understood in Foreign Parts.' Improvisations upon a bass were popular in the seventeenth and eighteenth centuries and other books appeared in England on the subject.[17] A third edition of the book appeared as late as 1712.

The Compendium; or, Introduction to Practical Music was Simpson's third and last theoretical work.

THE COMPENDIUM

Judging by the number of editions over such a lengthy period, the *Compendium* was more popular than *The Division-Viol*. In 1665, what may be considered to be the first edition of the *Compendium* was published with the title *The Principles of Practical Music delivered in a Compendious, Easie and New Method: For the Instruction of Beginners, either in Singing or Playing upon Instruments. To which are added Some Short and Easie Ayres designed for Learners. . . .* The book consisted of the first part of the *Compendium*, namely the 'Rudiments of Song,' and was dedicated to Sir John St. Barbe, Bart., 'part of it being framed for your instruction.' The second edition appeared in 1667 and contained the four other parts together with the 'Rudiments of Song' from the first edition, which was almost unchanged. Simpson acknowledges

---

[17] John Playford, *The Division Violin*, 1685. *The Division Flute*, Anon., 1722.

his obligations to Mathew Locke 'both for his suggestions and assistance in this treatise.'

Letters of commendation by Jenkins and Locke are included in this second edition. Locke's letter was not included in the third edition (1678), but the 'Short and Easie Ayres Designed for Learners' was appended. The fourth edition was published in 1706 and the fifth and sixth in 1714, although Grove's Dictionary gives 1722 as the date of the sixth edition.[18] There are minor alterations and omissions in these and in the seventh (1727) and the eighth (1732) editions. No date is given for the ninth; the British Museum Catalogue gives 1775 but Rimbault[19] mentions 1790.

So many editions of the *Compendium* over so long a period point to its considerable usefulness. The letters of commendation by two of the foremost composers of the day speak for themselves. Roger North was not quite so complimentary—and even less so about Playford's *Brief Introduction:*

> The book of Mr Morley hath sufficiently shewed the rules of musick in his time, but it is not easy to gather them out of his dialogue way of wrighting, which according to usage is stuft with abundance of impertinences, and also with matters, in our practise, wholly obsolete. I know many serve themselves of Mr Sympson's books, which are doubdtless very good, and worthy as could be expected from a meer musick master, as he was, but they are not compleat. Nay some make a shift with poor old Playford's *Introduction* of which may be truely sayd that it is but just (if at all) better than none. But there is a musicall grammer ever to be recomended, compiled by a learned man, and compleat in all grammatticall formes. It was put out by a famous master of sciences Mr Butler, and I doe not know another in any language comparable to it.[20]

Such disdain for Morley and Simpson, contempt for Playford and prejudice in favour of Butler does not speak well of North's judgement in this field.

Mace had a high regard for the *Compendium* and Simpson's other theoretical works. He writes in *Musick's Monument:*

> I shall refer you to Mr. Christopher Simpson's late and very Compleat Works: where you may inform yourself sufficiently in That Matter, who hath sav'd me a Labour therein; (for had It not been so Exactly done by Him, I should have said something to It, though (it may be) not so much to the Purpose).[21]

[18] The copy in the British Museum Catalogue is dated 1714, but Eitner gives the date 1722 in *Quellen-Lexicon*, Leipzig, IX (1903), 180.

[19] The Hon. Roger North, *Memoirs of Musick*, ed. by Edward F. Rimbault, London, 1846, p. 94n.

[20] John Wilson, ed., *op. cit.*, p. 137. See also J. A. Westrup, *Purcell*, London, 1937, p. 253.

[21] Mace, *op. cit.*, p. 217.

Purcell was critical of Simpson's rules but thought well of the book as a whole. He writes:

> The first Thing to treat of is Counter point, and in this I must differ from Mr. Simpson (whose Compendium I admire as the most Ingenious Book I e'er met with upon this Subject;) but his Rule in Three Parts for Counterpoint Is too strict, and destructive to good Air which ought to be preferr'd before such Nice Rules.[22]

Later on both Burney and Hawkins in their respective Histories pay special attention to Simpson's *Compendium*. Hawkins in particular must have been familiar with Simpson's books, as already mentioned. Burney was doubtful concerning the value of instruction books alone:

> Whoever expects to learn the whole principles of an art by a single book, or, indeed any number of books, without oral instruction, or great study, practice and experience, must be disappointed. This compendium, like most others of the kind, more frequently generates new doubts and perplexities, than removes the old. However, something is to be learned from most books; and what a student is unable to find in one, if out of reach of a master, must be sought in another.

It is only fair to point out, however, that Burney later writes:

> As far as it [the *Compendium*] goes, this work has considerable merit for its clearness and simplicity.[23]

There were no violent changes in musical style in the years during which the various editions of the *Compendium* appeared. The information contained within the book did not therefore become quickly out of date. But it is clear that throughout such a period of more than a hundred and twenty years, certain modifications would need to be made to keep abreast of musical developments. Some changes took place in the methods of writing music. The diamond-shaped notes of the early editions were replaced by round notes in the fourth edition (1706), and at the same time the use of the blackened semibreve disappeared. For the most part the examples themselves remained unaltered since the musical language did not change sufficiently to make them either incomprehensible or antiquated. They are so simple in the first three parts of the book as to be almost devoid of character. This no doubt helped to make the *Compendium* fashionable for many years after Simpson's death and may to some extent account for its general popularity. Its appeal must have largely resulted from the subjects which are treated in it. The fact that the *Compendium* competed successfully with so many new instruction books in the eighteenth century cannot be regarded as conclusive proof of its merits in view of the low standards achieved in many of these publications.

[22] Purcell, writing in Playford's *Brief Introduction to the Skill of Musick*, 14th ed., 1700, Part III, 'An Introduction to the Art of Descant or Composing Musick in Parts,' p. 143. See also footnote 15 on p. 24 and footnote 24 on p. 75.   [23] Charles Burney, *op. cit.*, pp. 422 and 473.

The Contents of the 'Compendium'

The book is divided into five parts, each of which, with the exception of the last, may be subdivided into sections.

I. The Rudiments of Song
   Chapters 1–4 Pitch
   Chapters 5–11 Time

II. The Principles of Composition
   Chapters 1–6 Basic essentials—Intervals, Concords, Cadences
   Chapters 7–15 Progression of Concords

III. The Use of Discords
   Chapters 1–7 Treatment of Discords
   Chapters 8–10 Division of the Octave

IV. The Form of Figurate Descant
   Chapters 1–8 Counterpoint
   Chapters 9–12 Fugue
   Chapters 13–15 Vocal and Instrumental Music

V. The Contrivance of Canon

It will be seen that the main headings, in most cases, adequately describe the contents of each part. Chapters 8–10 of Part III (Division of the Octave) and chapters 13–15 of Part IV (Vocal and Instrumental Music) might be described as digressions; but Simpson forestalls would-be critics in the Preface (paragraph 5) in case they consider chapters 8–10 of Part III superfluous. He was obviously determined to introduce this material into his book. The information contained in chapters 13–15 of Part IV had to be included if the book were to live up to its name.

A discussion of the sections of the *Compendium* listed above follows.

Part I, Chapters 1–4, Pitch

The book begins with an account of the scale, its degrees, and how these may be altered chromatically. It is to Simpson's credit that he does not include a detailed examination of the scale in chapter 1. He leaves this until Part III, chapter 8. Similarly the discussion of the greater and lesser semitones (Part III, chapters 9 and 10) could have been included in Part I, chapter 4, 'Tuning the Degrees of Sound,' but this is not done. Such complicated theories, if presented at the beginning of the book, would be likely to puzzle the novice, and the understanding of them at an early stage is unnecessary, as Simpson well knew. The information contained in chapter 2, 'Of Naming the Degrees of Sound,' is also kept to a minimum. Fortunately, the system of solmization was not as complex in Simpson's day as it had been sixty years earlier. It would, however, have been tempting to discuss the principles of solmization as practised earlier in the seventeenth century, but to do this would again have confused the beginner with cumbersome details. This desire to avoid the introduction of unnecessary material can be seen in the very first paragraph of the book where the author writes: 'These degrees are numbered by sevens. To speak of the mystery of that number were to deviate from the business in hand.' This presumably refers to an attempt to connect the scale with the planetary system which Simpson himself made in *The Division-Viol*, Part II, chapter 13.

Part I, Chapters 5–11, Time

The remainder of the first part of the *Compendium* is devoted to the subject of Time, beginning with the names of the notes, their relationships and durations (chapters 5–7). In chapter 5, Simpson is brief in his explanations of early notation, a subject on which he was evidently not very well informed.

In chapter 6, concerning the 'Ancient Moods,' he recognizes that he must now depart from his principle of avoiding obsolete information. His explanations are, however, brief and there is no attempt to define the meanings of Time and Prolation. This discussion of the Moods leads naturally to the Common Mood (Imperfect of the Less) so that ultimately explanations of the relationships of note values in duple time are given.

An example follows which is most helpful; notes longer than a crotchet are broken down into crotchets (see p. 11). This provides the reader with an opportunity to apply the information just treated as well as that given in chapters 1–4, since the example is melodic as well as rhythmic. On page 12 a similar example is given in which crotchets are broken down into quavers.

After a brief chapter on syncopation and another on rests, Simpson goes on to treat of triple time. Here his earlier mention of the Triple Moods is useful. The only time signatures which occur in the book are 3 and in the 'Appendix of Short and Easy Airs,' ¢. The signature 3 is applied to all triple rhythms, whether the time is $\frac{3}{1}$, $\frac{3}{2}$, $\frac{3}{4}$, or $\frac{6}{4}$.

Simpson's account of the use of the blackened semibreve (p. 15) would appear at first sight to include out-of-date information, but examples using such notation are in the Appendix. Such signs as $\frac{6}{4}$ and $\frac{3}{2}$ are treated as proportions (see footnote 27 of Part I), and since Simpson is anxious not to become involved in a scholarly discussion of mensural notation, the last chapter in Part I is kept as short as possible.

Part II, Chapters 1–6, Basic essentials—Intervals, Concords, Cadences

The requirements which would enable a would-be musician to set about the task of composition are given in a concise form, preceded in chapter 1 by a definition of counterpoint and a statement that the bass is the foundation 'upon which all musical composition is to be erected.' This short chapter is therefore significant. In the first place, Simpson declares that he is teaching counterpoint, yet curiously all his examples in the second part appear to be homophonic. This perhaps is due to some extent to the simplicity of the examples given; but as all the parts move together at the same time (note against note with only an occasional suspension) the style appears to be anything but contrapuntal. The origin of the word counterpoint, coming as it does from the Latin *Punctus contra punctum*, hints at an earlier meaning which was used to describe a style in which each note moved simultaneously with those of other parts and it is in this sense that Simpson uses it. In the second place, Simpson's statement that it is from the *bass* that 'we are to measure or compute all those distances or intervals which are requisite for the joining of other parts thereto' bespeaks a method which was comparatively new in theoretical concept. Morley in his *Plain and Easy Introduction*, 1597,[24] and Renaissance writers generally, calculated their intervals from the tenor. Simpson knew this, as he was fully conversant with Morley's book.[25] It must not be assumed that Simpson originated this novel theoretical approach. Coperario in his book *Rules How to Compose* (although never published), written *c.* 1610, also calculates his intervals from the bass.[26]

Chapters 2 and 3 deal with intervals and concords. Here the Renaissance theory persists. The combination of sounds to form triads as we know them was not accepted in the sixteenth century, and Simpson's teaching continues this tradition. Musical progressions are taught with reference to intervals and it is natural that in chapter 4 Simpson should therefore begin with two-part 'counterpoint,' explaining what is allowed, or not allowed when the various intervals move to other intervals. This is not fully treated here. A more detailed examination of the subject is given in Part IV, chapters 6–8. In Part II,

[24] Thomas Morley, *A Plain and Easy Introduction to Practical Music*, ed. by R. Alec Harman, London, 1952.
[25] Simpson writes in *The Division-Viol*, Part II: 'Although our excellent Country-man Mr. Morley, in his Introduction to Musick, doth take his sight, and reckon his Concords from the Tenor, as the Holding Part to which He and the Musicians of former times were accustomed to apply their Descant, in order to the Gregorian Musick of the Church; yet here, for better reasons (as to our present purpose) I must propose unto you the Bass, as the Groundwork or Foundation upon which all Musical Composition is to be erected; and from it we are to reckon or compute all those distances or Intervalls which we use in joyning Parts together.'
[26] Giovanni Coperario, *Rules How to Compose*, ed. by Manfred F. Bukofzer, Los Angeles, 1952. A facsimile edition of the Bridgewater MS.

Simpson is trying, with a minimum of explanation, to reach a stage where the reader will have the satisfaction of being able to compose his own music, and consequently the more advanced consideration of the movement of intervals is reserved for later discussion.

Greater continuity would have been achieved if Simpson had followed this by the chapter on 'How to Frame a Bass,' but two other subjects need to be considered beforehand. The first concerns key, in which Simpson uses the terms *sharp and flat key* to mean major and minor respectively and shows that modality has given way to tonality. This is yet another reason, incidentally, why Simpson's treatise lived on when many others died; 1667 is an early date to be theorizing on the key system, and the following chapter, 'Of the Closes or Cadences belonging to the key' reaffirms the suspicion that here is something unexpected in a theoretical treatise of this time. Admittedly the tonality is rudimentary; all the same, the opening sentence of this sixth chapter, 'Having spoken of the key or tone, it follows in order that we speak of the closes or cadences which belong unto it,' illustrates Simpson's understanding of the way in which tonal progressions move towards the cadence.

Part II, Chapters 7–15, Progression of Concords

The remainder of the second part of the book shows clearly Simpson's systematic approach. In nine short chapters he proceeds from the construction of a bass to eight-part writing, the instruction for 'Composition in Three Parts' being an ingenious account of how these concordant intervals may be used simultaneously to produce concords.

Having taught four-part writing, Simpson now calls a halt to this adding of parts to the same bass and introduces a new chord into the reader's vocabulary—the first inversion of the seventh chord. This also is taught by interval; in chapter 11 we read of 'How a 5th and 6th may stand together in Counterpoint.'

Since all the examples in chapters 7–10 are constructed on the same bass which is in a minor key, chapter 12 deals with the omission this has caused, 'Composition in a Sharp Key' (i.e. major key).

Before resuming his narrative, 'One thing yet remains, very necessary sometimes in composition' and that is passing notes (chapter 13). Chapters 14 and 15 achieve the object of teaching composition in five, six, seven and eight parts. The examples in chapter 14 (five, six and seven parts) are constructed so that each additional part is merely added to the parts of the previous example. All the examples in the last two chapters are in the major key, so as to retain a balance with the examples in two, three and four parts which were in the minor.

The modern approach to the writing of music in many parts is very different from Simpson's. It should not be thought that his attitude comes from a desire to demonstrate his own capabilities. At first sight it appears presumptuous that he should expect the reader to attempt eight-part writing after such a brief account. But the musical style chosen for his illustrations is very simple and the main difficulty, the avoidance of 'consecution of perfects of the same kind', is discussed.

Part III, Chapters 1–7, Treatment of Discords

Discords are taught by reference to intervals, the same method which Simpson used in the teaching of concords. He does not clearly describe how discordant intervals are to be combined with other concordant or discordant intervals to form discords. There is no chapter in Part III which corresponds to chapter 9 in Part II where a method of combining concordant intervals is to be found. Thus most of the examples teaching the use of discords are in two parts.

It will be remembered that certain discords have already been discussed in Part II—those formed by a suspension at the cadence (chapter 8) and those produced by 'breaking a note' (chapter 13). These two topics are reintroduced in Part III, chapters 2 and 3 in more detail. The chapter on suspensions is, however, very brief, much of the explanation being left to the examples themselves, though a list of those suspensions which may be employed is given.

It is perhaps unfortunate that Simpson moves from examples of discords in two parts to similar examples in three parts, 'but not one word of instruction how to make such like' (to use Simpson's own critical words of Elway Bevin's book). Chapter 4, 'Passage of Discords,' compensates to some extent for omissions in chapter 3, but there is still no systematic method employed. Suspensions in the bass are not treated individually, nor is there any mention of ornamental resolutions. Details concerning the preparation of suspended notes are also conspicuously absent. This is particularly noticeable in chapter 5 when a third method of introducing a discord is distinguished. The first two methods employ different note values in the individual parts. This third method employs notes 'of the same quantity against one another,' by which means true discords as we understand them can be created. This is, in fact, a simple study of the dominant seventh, disguised as a tritone or semidiapente. Only the first and last inversions of the chord appear (in the three-part example), but the customary rules are observed, the third rising, the seventh falling.

Chapter 6 is a supplement to chapter 2, describing how discords result from parts moving by passing notes to a concord. (It would be interesting to know how Simpson would have harmonized his examples in four parts.)

The section on discords now being complete, Simpson next treats the subject of false relation at some length.

Part III, Chapters 8–10, Division of the Octave

The rest of this part is concerned with an account of the theoretical aspects of the scale and with acoustics. It is clear that Simpson's misgivings as expressed in his Preface are to some extent well founded. The treatment of the subject is too short to allow for detailed explanations, so necessary in dealing with such a topic. The whole of the third part of his book would probably have been improved if this subject had been omitted and the space used to clarify the treatment of discords, particularly suspensions. No doubt Simpson felt obliged to discuss a subject which had received so much attention from earlier theorists and its inclusion helps to lend respectability to a book which was written with the object of being popular.

Part IV, Chapters 1–8, Counterpoint

It is in this part of the book that we should expect Simpson to excel in a discussion of one of his favourite subjects. As mentioned earlier, he was an authority on improvisations on a given theme, and it would be natural to assume that his account would illustrate his abilities to the full. Unfortunately a compendium of music does not allow space for enlarging upon ideas or providing details. As Simpson points out in the second paragraph of chapter 3, 'To give you models at large of all those several structures were to write a great volume, not a Compendium.' This section of the book, although having a certain charm, does not compare favourably with Part III of *The Division-Viol* where the same subject is treated in great detail.

The fact that Simpson devotes several chapters of his book to the teaching of ornamenting a simple melodic line does not only reflect his personal view. This art of elaboration was regarded as an important accomplishment which should occupy a major part of the student's attention and it was treated at length by theoretical writers of the day.[27]

The title of Part IV of the book leads the reader to assume that the whole section is devoted to this subject. But after the short first chapter which defines the practice of figurate descant, the next chapter, entitled 'Of the Greek Modes and Latin Tones,' deals with the church modes in a rather haphazard way.

---

[27] A list of those books which deal with the subject is to be found in an article by Manfred F. Bukofzer, 'On the performance of Renaissance music,' in *Proceedings of the Music Teachers National Association*, Series 36, 1941, p. 225.

A return to the main subject is made in the third chapter, and the next two chapters also instruct the reader on how to form figurate descant. Since much detail is omitted, the teaching assumes a more general character, relying on information already given and also on the examples. There is no attempt to discuss the nature of the moving parts, or to show which figures will fit best between certain chords. The substance of the text is even trivial, but it is the examples which keep alive the interest. Reliance is also placed on chapter 13 of Part II: 'Of Transition, or Breaking a Note,' although the reader is not reminded to consult this. Instead it is suggested that he should refer 'to the principles formerly delivered in composition of two parts,' presumably the first eight chapters of the second part. The absence of detail results in a simple text, appropriate to the demands of the beginner.

In chapters 6–8 there is a return to the earlier approach of examples illustrating specific points in the text. These deal with the 'consecution' of various intervals. This subject has been treated in Part II, chapter 4, but now requires further attention in view of what has been taught in the previous chapters. Forbidden consecutives are more likely to pass unobserved in florid counterpoint than in the note against note style of Part II.

Part IV, Chapters 9–12, Fugue

His teaching method consists of the provision of comprehensive examples together with a general commentary in the text, and the choice of subject is the natural outcome of what has already been explained. These chapters must have been of considerable interest to serious amateurs for they teach the construction of the Fancy, which according to Simpson was the chief form of instrumental music, although he regrets that it 'is now much neglected, by reason of the scarcity of auditors that understand it.'

After acquainting the reader with various kinds of 'fugue' (chapters 9–11), Simpson adopts a method of teaching in chapter 12, 'How to form a Fugue,' which is both instructive and clear. The individual points are set down in the various parts in his 'Example of the first platform of a fugue' and the reader is instructed on how to complete and extend the composition. This method is used again in Part V.

Part IV, Chapters 13–15, Vocal and Instrumental Music

The last three chapters of Part IV briefly describe the forms of vocal and instrumental music of the time with a certain emphasis on arrangement and word-setting. Simpson also advocates the copying of the works of well-known composers ('that they may serve you as a pattern to imitate') is of value to the student.

Part V, Canon

As Simpson took no model on which to base his account (as he says himself, 'none that I meet with have published any instructions for making a canon') the result is admirable.

The first chapter is concerned with the definition of canon, and since there is a lack of written instruction on how to construct a canon, 'our business must be to try what helps we can afford a learner.' Simpson's reasons for considering the subject of canon sufficiently important to warrant a fifth share in his treatise are not fully stated. He merely says that, 'the exercise thereof will much enable you in all other kinds of composition, especially where anything of fugue is concerned.' Quite possibly this is hinting that an understanding of the ways in which canon is constructed might enable a reader of the time to compose a Catch or Round. This was a popular form during the seventeenth and eighteenth centuries and set to verses which, through being broken up by the different parts into words and phrases, resulted frequently in amusing and sometimes indecent associations. It is interesting to note that although Simpson disapproved of the Catch, the last chapter of his book is devoted to this vocal form.

In the last sentence of chapter 1 the reader is informed of Simpson's intention to teach canon 'in the same method which I did before in contriving a single fugue, that is, first to set down your material notes and then to accommodate your other descant to those notes.' This, together with his careful analysis of the various types of canon which are taught in order of complexity, produces an easily followed narrative, moving from a simple canon in two parts to a canon at the 13th set against a plainsong.

Summary

It is evident from the text and general layout of the *Compendium* that in spite of various shortcomings, many of the requirements of a book designed to furnish a beginner with an understanding of fundamental principles are satisfied. No previous knowledge is assumed and the reader is not puzzled by detailed explanations in the early stages, by obscure discussion and by out-of-date theories (with minor exceptions). The book is addressed directly to the student, and is not intended primarily for the use of the teacher actually giving instruction. The most recent theories are employed, such as the measuring of intervals from the bass and at all times explanations are kept to a minimum of words. In the choice and presentation of material, a suitable balance is maintained between what the reader wants to know and what he must be taught. In the fifth part of the book, for example, the reader must be taught the intricacies of canon before he is able to compose a Catch. The treatment throughout is systematic, proceeding from the simple to the complex. An understanding of subsequent parts of the book is dependent on the previous parts and a reader cannot begin Part II until he has mastered Part I. These various parts represent stages in musical ability which, when achieved, give a certain satisfaction to the reader. Having mastered Part I he is able to sing a part at sight. Having mastered Part II, he is able to compose music using concords; from Part III he can learn to use discords. Part IV teaches him to compose a Fancy, and Part V a Canon or a Catch. The book is full of musical examples, some charming, all informative. Sometimes these examples illustrate points made in the text; at other times it is the musical examples which explain the procedure, the text merely serving to describe the examples.

It is perhaps disappointing that Simpson teaches no more than is necessary to achieve a desired purpose, as is the case with teaching of florid counterpoint in Part III, but there is no space for either reflection or loquacity. Simpson felt bound to write the book, as he says in his Preface, and to make it as concise and comprehensible as possible. Although some obsolete theories appear from time to time, he attempts to dismiss them whenever possible by such sentences as, 'The other two, Ut and Re, are superfluous and therefore laid aside by most modern teachers.' There is no wish to delve into scholarly abstractions. Simpson is not demonstrating his musical skill; he is 'communicating his knowledge to others,' using his gift for making difficult and complicated subjects appear easy and simple.

THE 'COMPENDIUM' AND THE INSTRUCTION BOOK TRADITION

Public interest in music continued to grow throughout the second half of the seventeenth century. England had emerged from the austerity of the Interregnum seven years before the complete edition of the *Compendium* was published, but the early years of the Restoration period were not propitious. After 1666, the return to national prosperity was marked by an increase and considerable deployment of wealth, evident in such things as new architectural and cultural ventures.[28] It is most likely that Simpson's book was addressed to the classes who were trying to better themselves and to enjoy some of the privileges previously denied them. The public interest in Restoration comedy, which frequently included songs and incidental music, developed into a taste for opera and oratorio in Handel's day. As early as 1672 public concerts were being given and the number of them

[28] John Harley, art. 'Music and Musicians in Restoration London,' in *Musical Quarterly*, XL (1954), 509.

greatly increased in the eighteenth century. Musical life was thus established and maintained among the middle classes, although dominated in the eighteenth century by foreign musicians.

The growing interest in music throughout this period is reflected in the increasing number of musical publications in England. 1651, the date of Playford's original *English Dancing Master*, marks the beginning of a 'revival' of printed music books, the previous thirty years being rather barren in publications of this kind. Playford's business continued to flourish after his death in 1686 when his son, Henry, succeeded to it. In the eighteenth century, printed music was supplied in great quantity by firms such as that of John Walsh, Handel's publisher. In this way, a supply of printed music was organized to meet the public demands for this commodity.

The publication of instruction books was a means of creating and encouraging an interest in music and thereby increasing the public demand for the sale of printed music. Consequently it is not surprising that so many instruction books appeared in England in the seventeenth and eighteenth centuries. The gradually expanding market frequently called for new editions of old instruction books, suitably amended to conform with musical developments. Simpson's *Compendium* was one of these which managed to hold its own in the face of new publications in the same field. This betokens a popularity which is dependent not only upon the contents of the book, but also upon the relative merits of other instruction books.

Instruction books before 1667

Those instruction books written in the earlier part of the seventeenth century were going out of date when Simpson wrote his *Compendium*. Morley's *Plain and Easy Introduction to Practical Music*, published in 1597, had served a useful purpose and may be regarded as the first of these instruction books in English. Morley's book teaches how to compose music in Renaissance style and it was therefore becoming obsolete in the 1660s. In Morley's work, as has been said, intervals are calculated from the tenor, and much of his advice must have baffled the limited musical understanding of the novice. No doubt Morley desired to acquaint his readers with information which he had been to great lengths to acquire and also to air his command of musical scholarship,[29] although no previous musical knowledge on the part of the reader is assumed. Simpson makes several references to Morley in the *Compendium*.

[29] See the Foreword by R. Thurston Dart to R. A. Harman's edition of Morley's *Plain and Easy Introduction*, p. xxi.

Thomas Robinson's *A Schoole of Music*, 1603, and Ravenscroft's *A Brief Discourse of the True (but Neglected) Use of Charact'ring by Degrees*, 1618, were probably not helpful to Simpson in his work on the *Compendium*. The former is an instrumental tutor, and the latter, a dissertation on 'Divisions of Moode, Time and Prolation in Measurable Music.' Perhaps the most important instruction book to follow Morley's was *A New Way of Making Fowre Parts in Counter-Point*, 1613, by Thomas Campion. By 1655 it was sufficiently out of date to require Simpson's explanations in the text.

Charles Butler's *The Principles of Musik, in Singing and Setting (Ecclesiastical and Civil)*, 1636, is a profound piece of scholarship but difficult for the musical beginner. The text is not designed to convey the reader from the simple to the complex; and the long quotations in Latin and Greek (not to mention Butler's attempted reforms of English orthography) are hardly conducive to easy reading.

Elway Bevin's treatise of 1631 teaches much more than Simpson's reference to it would lead us to believe. Its full title is *A Brief and Short Instrvction of the Art of Mvsicke to teach how to make Discant of all proportions that are in vse: very necessary for all such as are desirous to attaine to knowledge in the Art; and may by practice, if they can sing, soone be able to compose three, foure and five parts: And also to compose all sorts of Canons that are usuall, by these directions of two or three parts in one, upon a Plainsong*. Burney remarks that, 'however useless it [Bevin's book] may be deemed now, [it] must have been of singular service to young students in times when canons were regarded as the greatest efforts of human intellect, and the solution of these enigmas was equally difficult with that of the most abstruse and complicated problems in Euclid.'[30] Simpson also refers to Descartes' *Compendium of Music* which was translated into English by Viscount Brouncker and published in 1653. This is a scholarly philosophical discussion, mainly on the nature of intervals (up to chapter 12), with a chapter entitled, 'Of the reason of composing' (although actual problems of how to compose are avoided) and one on the modes. There are only a few musical examples, though plenty of diagrams. Descartes' work can hardly be described as an instruction book; though it is a theoretical treatise which discusses elementary subjects in a profound way. Similarly Athanasius Kircher's *Musurgia Universalis*, 1650, which is also mentioned by Simpson, was not likely to be of much value to a beginner because of its approach and the advanced nature of the speculation Kircher engages in.

Of those books published prior to the appearance of the *Compendium*, the one with the greatest similarity to Simpson's is John Playford's *A Brief Introduction to the Skill of Music*, first published in

---

[30] Burney, *op. cit.*, III (1789), 328.

1654. This little book, which went into innumerable editions until 1730, was written by Playford with the probable intention of furthering his music-selling business. The verse which appears in the book is perhaps an attempt to disguise Playford's commercial interests:

> This Playford's shadow doth present,
> Peruse his Booke and there you'll see,
> His whole designe is Publique Good,
> His Soule and Minde an Harmonie.

The book is a collection of information on musical subjects rather than a systematic method of how to acquire knowledge of composition. Part I is 'The Grounds and Rules of Musick according to the Gam-ut and other principles thereof.' Part II gives 'Instructions for the Bass Viol and also for the Treble-Violin with Lessons for beginners'; and the last part is 'The Art of Setting, or Composing of Musick in Parts by Dr. Tho. Campion, with Annotations thereon by Mr. C. Simpson,' which is itself in three parts. Other subjects are treated than those listed on the title-page. There is 'A brief Discourse of and Directions for Singing after the Italian manner . . . Written some years since by an English Gentleman who had lived in Italy . . .' and also 'The Tunes of the Psalmes. . . .' The commercial advantages of putting so many topics together in one book is clear. However, this work was not a very expensive one; even in 1706 it was selling at only 2s. a copy.

Another small book which appeared in 1664, one year before the first edition of the *Compendium*, was a translation by John Birchensha of the section 'Musica' from Alstedt's *Scientiarum omnium Encyclopaedia*, 1610, under the title *Templum Musicum*. This, as the title announces, is a *Compendium of the Rudiments both of the Mathematical and Practical Part of Musick*. The book is not intended for those who wish to learn counterpoint and composition; as the title suggests, its main emphasis falls on the mathematical aspects of music.

These, then, are some of the instruction books which Simpson may have known and used as models in the writing of his *Compendium or Introduction to Practical Music*. We have proof that he knew at least six of them. In these can be seen features which Simpson adopted for his own use, and many others which he rejected as unnecessary in the construction of his simple methodical work. Simpson does not have recourse to the witty asides such as we find in Morley's famous work; but he frequently draws upon Morley for explanations of certain procedures which he himself finds it difficult to give. This shows Simpson's respect for Morley, a respect which he possibly had also for Descartes, although it is obvious that Simpson had no wish to imitate the erudite style of the French philosopher. The idea of devoting a complete section of his book to the subject of canon must have been the result of studying Elway Bevin's work. Similarly, the inclusion of information concerning the vibrations of a divided string was probably made after reading parts of *Musurgia Universalis*. But it is from two books not quoted in the *Compendium* that Simpson drew many ideas. The portion of Playford's book devoted to the treatment of rudiments was probably used by Simpson as a model for the first part of the *Compendium*. The simple language is characteristic of both; the subjects are the same and their treatment is similar. Simpson's second main source was the Campion essay which he annotated for inclusion in Playford's *Brief Introduction*. The general layout of this essay was adopted by Simpson for his own use. Many examples are to be found in Campion's work which are in note against note style with numbers indicating the size of the intervals measured from the bass. Simpson also made use in the *Compendium* of his own annotations to Campion's essay. In a footnote on the first page to Campion's chapter heading, 'Of Counterpoint,' Simpson writes, 'And, because in Plain-song Musick we set Note against Note, as they did Point against Point, thence it is, that this kind of Musick doth still retain the name of Counterpoint.' This passage corresponds closely with the first paragraph of the second part of the *Compendium*, and several other instances of the same kind may be seen. For example, in the annotations to Campion's work Simpson writes: 'By their Compounds is meant their Octaves, as a third and its eighths, a fifth and its eighths, etc.'; this is very similar to passages in both the *Compendium* (p. 20) and *The Division-Viol*.

Another source of information for the *Compendium* was Simpson's own earlier book. When he says in the Preface to the *Compendium*, 'I have taken some parcels out of a book I formerly published to make up this Compendium,' he is of course referring to *The Division-Viol*. Some passages in the second and third parts of the *Compendium* are taken from the second part of *The Division-Viol*. Chapter headings are frequently the same, as is the material treated under them, but the wording frequently differs and Simpson wrote new musical examples for the *Compendium*. The changed wording may be accounted for by the fact that Simpson was explaining the same topics to readers whose interests differed—the practical musician on the one hand, the general student of music on the other. However, in the majority of cases, the explanations in the *Compendium* are much more thorough, and Simpson is at pains to leave no doubts in the reader's mind. Two corresponding passages from the two books, which may be compared with the above quotation from his notes on Campion's essay, will serve to illustrate this. In *The Division-Viol* he writes: 'Concords are these; a Third, a Fifth, a Sixth, an Eighth and their Octaves,' and in the *Compendium*:

'Concords in Musick are these, 3d, 5th, 6th, 8th. By which I also mean their Octaves; as 10th, 12th, 13th, 15th, etc.'[31] The possible explanation for the fact that similarities such as this occur in all three books may be that Simpson also made use of the Campion essay and his own annotations upon it when he was writing *The Division-Viol*.

The whole undertaking of the *Compendium* was perhaps in response to some lines written by Playford which appear in his *Brief Introduction*:

> Therefore when I had considered the great want of Books of this Divine Art of Musick in our own language, it was a great motive to me to undertake this Work, though I must confess our nation is at this time plentifully stored with learned and skilful men in this science, better able than myself to have undertaken this Task; but their slowness and modesty (being, as I conceive unwilling to appear in print about so small a matter) has made me adventure on it, though with the Danger of not being so well done as they might have performed it; the rather induced thereunto, for that the Prescription of Rules of all Arts and Sciences ought to be delivered in plain and brief language, and not in flowers of eloquence; which Maxime I have followed: For after the most brief, plain and easie method I could invent, I have here set down the Grounds of Musick, . . .

Instruction books after 1667

It is an interesting thought that the *Compendium* was apparently as useful to music students in the days of ~~John~~ Jenkins as it was to those in the time of Blow, Purcell, Arne, Webbe and Samuel Wesley. But it was inevitable that as musical style changed, the book must eventually fall short of the demands of the reader. Changing theoretical concepts in the eighteenth century such as those outlined in Rameau's *Traité de l'harmonie*, 1722, diminished its usefulness. The third part of Rameau's work was translated into English and published in 1752 under the title of *A Treatise of Musick, Containing the Principles of Composition* and this date may well mark the fall from favour of the *Compendium or Introduction to Practical Music*. Only the ninth edition was published after this date and this was an attempt to give Simpson's book a new lease of life by changing the wording, supplying footnotes, modernizing the spelling and the musical examples and generally bringing it up to date. This did not affect the natural course of events, however, and no tenth edition of the *Compendium* was published.

It is difficult to estimate the influence which the *Compendium* had on subsequent instruction books. After all, the ways in which elementary subjects can be treated is necessarily somewhat limited. Many instruction books fall short of the standards achieved by Simpson and do not attempt to cover such a wide range of subjects as he did. From Simpson's own time there was a tendency towards specialization as is

---

[31] The *Compendium*, Part II, chapters 2–5, 7–10, and Part III, chapters 2–5 are comparable with *The Division-Viol*, Part II chapters 2–12.

shown by books teaching the practice of figured bass, such as Locke's *Melothesia, or Certain Rules for playing upon a Continued Bass*, 1673, and by books teaching harmony—*A Treatise of the Natural Grounds and Principles of Harmony*, 1694, by William Holder, D.D. (with only one musical example in the whole book). Edward Betts's *Introduction to the Skill of Music*, 1724, briefly describes the rudiments, but the rest of the book is an anthology of anthems and hymn tunes by Blow, Purcell and others; the diagram on page 1 of Betts's book, showing the Gamut, is practically identical with that on page 1 of Simpson's book and it is likely (but by no means certain) that Betts made use of the *Compendium*. Simpson's influence on William Tansur, who in 1746 published *A New Musical Grammar*, is perhaps more clearly seen, but difficult to prove. The book teaches rudiments and composition by the master-scholar dialogue method. It covers much of Simpson's ground in the early stages and then deals with instruments—the flute, violin and organ. Tansur returns to Simpson's material, mentioning the division of a string into equal parts and teaching the rules of composition beginning with two parts. Chapter II has the title, 'Composition in 5, 6 and 7 parts,' which is almost the same as one of Simpson's chapter headings and Tansur's book ends with the teaching of fugue and canon. Dr. Pepusch also ends his *Short Treatise on Harmony*, 1730, with a final chapter on fugue and canon. Robert Bremner's *The Rudiments of Music*, published in Edinburgh in 1756, certainly owes much to the first part of the *Compendium*. Bremner's opening chapter, 'Of the Scale,' reads:

It is the End and Office of the Scale to shew the Degrees of Sound, by which a Voice may melodiously either ascend or descend to any harmonical Distance.

These degrees are in Number seven, and are distinguished by the first seven letters of the Alphabet. . . .

A comparison between the above quotation and the opening paragraphs of the *Compendium* shows that Bremner has merely reproduced Simpson's original text. Bremner's rule for placing Mi is the same as Simpson's; he also appropriated Simpson's chapter, 'Of Keeping Time.'

Musicians were at last discovering that it was not in their best interests to baffle their readers with mathematics. John De La Fond specifically points to this in the title of his book, *A New System of Music both Theoretical and Practical and yet not Mathematical*, 1725, which is mainly philosophical and can hardly be called a manual of instruction. However, treatises dealing with the mathematical basis of music still continued to appear, one being published only a year later in 1726 with the title, *A Preliminary Discourse to a Scheme Demonstrating and Shewing the Perfection and Harmony of Sounds*, by William Jackson, M.M.

Two books which achieve a good standard are Alexander Malcolm's *Treatise of Music*, 1776, and William Jones's *Treatise on the Art of Music*, 1784. Malcolm's work is not an instruction book of the Simpson type, but adheres more to the realms of theoretical speculation and musical history. Jones's theories on harmony are not so advanced as those of Rameau, but he nevertheless attempts a methodical approach to the subject.

It will be seen that many of the instruction books in English in the eighteenth century frequently leave much to be desired. Books such as *A Complete System of Harmony*, 1768, by John Heck, a German living in London, are all too few. He deals with his material under such headings as 'Of the Common Chord, Of the First Inversion of the Common Chord, Of the Second Inversion of the same, Of the Chord of the Seventh, Of the Chord of the Ninth,' showing a treatment of the subject in the most modern terms. This book, however, is still limited in its scope when compared with the *Compendium* for it confines itself only to the rules of harmony.

There can be no doubt that Christopher Simpson's *Compendium or Introduction to Practical Music* was influential in furthering the knowledge of music in the seventeenth and eighteenth centuries, rivalling and outliving even Playford's *Brief Introduction*. Few subsequent books improved upon it; even less could they compare with its wealth of material and brevity. It was thus permitted to grow old gracefully and to die at a great age from natural causes. When Simpson's compositions are more widely known, he may be allowed to join that distinguished gathering of English composers (Morley, Dowland, Coperario, Locke, Blow, Purcell and many more) who devoted some of their time to the instruction of others, even though, according to Roger North, the author of the *Compendium* was but 'a meer musick master.'

G. Carwarden pinxit.   ·VBIQUE LUX SINE VMBRA·   Guil. Faithorne sculp:

Christophori Simpson Effigies.

Christopher Simpson (an engraving from the 1955 facsimile edition of Simpson's *The Division-Viol*).

Reproduced by permission of J. Curwen and Sons Ltd.,

A
COMPENDIUM
OF
PRACTICAL MUSICK

IN FIVE PARTS:

Teaching, by a New, and easie Method,

1. *The Rudiments of Song.*
2. *The Principles of Composition.*
3. *The Use of Discords.*
4. *The Form of Figurate Descant.*
5. *The Contrivance of Canon.*

By CHRISTOPHER SIMPSON.

Cantate Domino Canticum novum :
Laus ejus in Ecclesia Sanctorum.

Pf. 149.

London , Printed by *William Godbid* for *Henry Brome*
in *Little Britain.* M. DC. LXVII.

The Title-page of the Second Edition of the *Compendium* (1667).
reprinted by kind permission of the Manchester Public Libraries.

To the truly Noble, Magnanimous and Illustrious PRINCE

WILLIAM CAVENDISH

Duke, Marquis, and Earl of Newcastle; Earl of Ogle; Viscount Mansfield; and Baron of Bolsover, of Ogle, Bothal and Hepple; Gentleman of His Majesty's Bed-chamber; One of His Majesty's most Honourable Privy Council, Knight of the most Noble Order of the Garter; His Majesty's Lieutenant of the County and Town of Nottingham; and Justice in Ayre Trent-North, etc.

MY LORD,

The benign aspect which your Grace doth cast upon this science by cherishing and maintaining such as are excellent in it, as also your particular favours to myself and your being pleased with some things which I formerly composed for your Grace's recreation, have given me the confidence of presenting to your Grace this little treatise. It is but a Compendium, my Lord, yet contains all that is requisite to the knowledge of practical music. And I must needs think it very fortunate in its nativity that it comes into the world in such a time as to find in one individual person so illustrious a patron to protect it, and so able a judge to understand it, your Grace, in younger years, having been so eminent in the same art. Which, I hope, does no way derogate from your honour since kings, as well as subjects, have thought it no disparagement to be counted skilful in the art of music.

The Muses have always been your handmaids, my Lord, as may be seen in divers of your excellent poems; but your Grace has only cast some amorous glances upon them, your active genius finding out other more strenuous and heroic divertisments; witness that incomparable and elaborate treatise of managing and riding the great horse and teaching that useful and docile creature all the postures and exercises which nature hath made him capable of, for the service of man in all occasions of war and peace. As also your most exquisite skill and dexterity at your weapon which have rendered your name famous, not only in our own, but in foreign nations. Those things, my Lord, which you have left in writing will remain as signal monuments of your name and memory when your titles and estate shall be transferred to your posterity.

The time is yet fresh in each one's memory when this kingdom was in so high a distemper that every loyal subject was bound in duty to equip himself for the defence of his king and country, and then, my Lord, I had the honour to serve under your Grace's command when you were general of the gallantest army that I think was ever raised in these dominions by the industry of any one single person, and therefore very properly styled, your army. If others by your example had shown the like loyalty, gallantry and industry, those rugged times had come to a shorter period.

I should not have mentioned these things, my Lord, had it not been to show with how much reason (if I had anything worthy of acceptance) I stand obliged to offer it at your Grace's feet, not only as a debt or duty on my part, but as a homage justly due unto your most eminent worth and merits; and this, I hope, will in some sense absolve me from the imputation of too much boldness in this dedication, since I had no better way to manifest myself, that I am,

My Lord,

Your Grace's most humble and truly devoted servant,

CHR. SIMPSON

TO THE READER[1]

THE esteem I ever had for Mr. Simpson's person and morals has not engaged me in any sort of partiality to his works, but I am yet glad of any occasion wherein I may fairly speak a manifest truth to his advantage and at the same time do a justice to the dead and a service to the living.

This Compendium of his I look upon as the clearest, the most useful and regular method of introduction to music that is yet extant. And herein I do but join in a testimony with greater judges. This is enough said on the behalf of a book that carries in itself its own recommendation.

ROGER L'ESTRANGE

[1] This letter first appears in the 3rd edition.

LICENSED, June 5th, 1667

ROGER L'ESTRANGE

THE PREFACE

I HAVE always been of opinion that if a man had made any discovery by which an art or science might be learnt with less expense of time and travail[2] he was obliged in common duty to communicate the knowledge thereof to others. This is the chief (if not only) motive which hath begot this little treatise.

And though I know a man can scarcely write upon any subject of this nature but the substance will be the same in effect which hath been taught before, yet thus much I may affirm, that the method is new, and (as I hope) both plain and easy. And some things also are explained which I have not seen mentioned in any former author.

I must acknowledge I have taken some parcels out of a book I formerly published to make up this *Compendium*, but I hope it is no felony to rob oneself,[3] this being intended for such as have no occasion to use the other. Also the first part of this book was printed by itself upon a particular occasion, but with intention and intimation of adding the other parts thereto, so soon as they were ready for the press, and the press for them.

Every man is pleased with his own conceptions, but no man can deliver that which shall please all men. Some perhaps will be dissatisfied with my method in teaching the principles of composition, the use of discords, and figurate descant in three distinct discourses which other commonly teach together promiscuously, but I am clearly of opinion that the principles of composition are best established in plain counterpoint, and the use of discords must be known before figurate descant can be formed.

Others may object that I fill up several pages with things superfluous, as namely my discourse of greater and lesser semitones and my showing that all the concords and other intervals of music arise from the division of a line or string into equal parts which are not the concern of practical music. 'Tis granted; but my demonstrations of them are practical, and though some do not regard such things, yet others, I doubt not, will be both satisfied and delighted with the knowledge of them.

If this which I now exhibit shall any way promote or facilitate the art of music, of which I profess myself a zealous lover, I have obtained the scope of my desires and the end of my endeavours. Or if any man else by my example shall endeavour to render it yet more easy, which I heartily wish, I shall be glad that I gave some occasion thereof. There

---

[2] Altered to 'time and travel' in the 3rd and subsequent editions.
[3] In all other editions this reads 'but I hope it is no theft to make use of one's own.'

is no danger of bringing music into contempt upon that account. The better it is known and understood, the more it will be valued and esteemed, and those that are most skilful may still find new occasions, if they please, to improve their knowledge in it.

I will not detain you too long in my Preface, only let me desire you first, to read over the whole discourse that you may know the design of it. Next, when you begin where you have occasion for instruction (if you desire to be instructed by it) that you make yourself perfect in that particular (and so, of each other) before you proceed to the next following, by which means your progress in it will be both more sure and more speedy. Lastly, that you receive it with the like candour and integrity with which it is offered to you, by

Your friend and servant,

C. S.

To his honoured friend, Mr. Christopher Simpson.

SIR,

I have with curious diligence perused your excellent *Compendium* and am infinitely satisfied with your method, it being both new, plain and rational, omitting nothing necessary nor adding anything super-fluous. And though perchance our new lights (of which this age has been monstrous fruitful) who can speculate how many hairs' breadths will reach from the top of Paul's steeple to the centre of a full moon and demonstrate that the thousandth part of a minute after, there will be so many thousand more hairs necessary by reason of the earth's or moon's motion; yet we poor practical men, who do because we do (as they are pleased to censure us) are content with such rules and predicaments only as are or may be useful to us, or such whose genius incline that way, leaving the rest to those who love to busy themselves about nothing, or to no purpose; of whom I shall make bold to deliver this truth, that I could never yet see that done by them which they pretend to be most versed in, viz. the production of ayre, which, in my opinion, is the soul of music. Thus, Sir, you have both my sentiment and thanks for your kind communication, and withal my hearty wishes that your ingenuous labours may receive that encourage-ment and reward which it really merits.

Sir,

June 1st 1667.   Your affectionate friend and humble servant,

MATT. LOCKE
Composer in Ordinary to His Majesty

To his much honoured and very precious friend, Mr. Christopher
    Simpson.

SIR,

Having perused your excellent *Compendium of Music* so far as my time and your pressing occasion could permit, I confess it my greatest concern to thank you for the product of so ingenious a work as tends to the improvement of the whole frame (I mean as to the least and most knowing capacities in the rudiments of that science). To speak in a word, the subject, matter, method, the platform and rational materials wherewith you raise and beautify this piece are such as will erect a lasting monument to the author and oblige the world as much to serve him, as he that is,

Sir,

Your most affectionate friend and servant,

JOHN JENKINS

TO ALL LOVERS OF HARMONY[4]

PRINCES of order, whose eternal arms
Puts chaos into concord, by whose charms,
The Cherubims in anthems clear and even
Create a consort for the King of Heaven;
Inspire me with thy magic, that my numbers
May rock the never-sleeping soul in slumbers:
Tune up my lyre, that when I sing thy merits,
My subdivided notes may sprinkle spirits
Into my auditory, whilst their fears
Suggest their souls are sallying through their ears...
What tropes and figures can thy glory reach,
That art thyself the splendour of all speech!
Mysterious music! He that doth thee right
Must show thy excellence by thine own light;
Thy purity must teach us how to praise—
As men seek out the sun with his own rays.
What creature that hath being, life, or sense,
But wears the badges of thine influence?
Music is harmony whose copious bounds
Is not confined only unto sounds;
'Tis the eyes object for (without extortion)
It comprehends all things that have proportion.
Music is concord, and doth hold allusion
With everything that doth oppose confusion.
In comely architecture it may be
Known by the name of uniformity;
Where pyramids to pyramids relate,
And the whole fabric doth configurate;
In perfectly proportion'd creatures we
Accept it by the title Symmetry:
When many men for some design convent,
And all concentre, it is call'd Consent:
Where mutual hearts in sympathy do move,
Some few embrace it by the name of Love:
But where the soul and body do agree
To serve their God, it is Divinity:
In all melodious compositions we
Declare and know it to be Symphony:

[4] This poem first appears in the 3rd edition

Where all the parts in complication roll,
And every one contributes to the whole,
He that can set and humour notes aright
Will move the soul to sorrow, to delight,
To courage, courtesy, to consolation,
To love, to gravity, to contemplation:
It hath been known (by its magnetic motion)
To raise repentance, and advance devotion.
It works on all the faculties, and why?
The very soul itself is harmony.
Music! it is the breath of second birth,
The saints employment and the angels mirth;
The rhetoric of Seraphims; a gem
In the King's crown of new Jerusalem:
They sing continually; the exposition
Must needs infer, there is no intermission.
I hear, some men hate music; let them show
In holy writ what else the angels do:
Then those that do despise such sacred mirth
Are neither fit for heaven, nor for earth.

PROEM

THE object of this science is sound, and that sound is two ways to be considered; as first, whether grave or acute. Secondly, whether long or short as to duration of time. The first of these is regulated by the scale of music; the latter by certain notes, marks or signs invented for that purpose. And these two, called tune and time, are the subject of the first part of this treatise and the foundation upon which the other parts are raised. The second part shows how grave and acute sounds are joined together in musical concordance. The third part brings discords into harmony, and out of these two, viz. concords and discords, is formed the fourth part named Figurate Descant. The fifth part leads Figurate Descant into Canon which is the culmen or highest degree of musical composition.

THE FIRST PART

TEACHING THE RUDIMENTS OF SONG

I. OF THE SCALE OF MUSIC

THE end and office of the scale of music is to show the degrees by which a voice, natural or artificial, may either ascend or descend. These degrees are numbered by sevens. To speak of the mystery of that number were to deviate from the business in hand. Let it suffice that music may be taught by any names of things so the number of seven be observed in ascending or descending by degrees.

Our common scale, to mark or distinguish those seven degrees, makes use of the same seven letters which in the calendar denote the seven days of the week, viz. A, B, C, D, E, F, G, after which follow

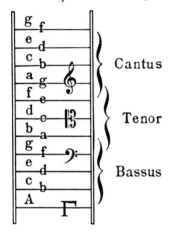

A, B, C, etc., over again, so often repeated as the compass of music doth require. The order of those letters is such as you see in the adjoined scale, to wit, in ascending we reckon them forward, in descending, backward. Where note, that every eighth letter, together with its degree of sound (whether you reckon upward or downward) is still the like, as well in nature as denomination. Together with these letters, the scale consists of lines and spaces, each line and each space being a several degree as you may perceive by the letters standing in them.

Those letters are called Clefs, Claves or Keys[1] because they open to us the meaning of every song.

On the lowest line is commonly placed this Greek letter *Γ* which Guido Arentius[2], who reduced the Greek scale into this form, did place at the bottom to signify from whence he did derive it, and from that letter the scale took the name of Gamma or Gam-ut.

On the middle of the scale you see three of those letters in different characters, of which some one is set at the beginning of every song. The lowest of them is the F clef, marked thus, 𝄢 which is peculiar

---

[1] Simpson writes *cliff*. In each case I have used clef. The word *claves* refers to *claves signatae* which in mediaeval theory meant the clef sign. *Clavis* is the Latin for key.

[2] Guido of Arezzo (b. 995). Selections of Guido's writings are contained in *Source Readings in Music History*, ed. by Oliver Strunk, London, 1952.

to the bass. The highest is a G clef made thus, ≡⬤≡ [3] and signifies the treble or highest part. Betwixt these two stands the C clef marked thus, ≣ which is a fifth below the G clef and a fifth also above the F clef, as you may observe by counting the degrees in the scale, reckoning both the terms inclusively. This clef standing in the middle serves for all inner parts.

When we see any one of these we know thereby what part it is and also what letters belong to each line and space which, though (for brevity) not set down at large, are notwithstanding supposed to be in those five lines and spaces in such order and manner as they stand in the scale itself.

EXAMPLE

Bass   Inner Part   Treble

2. Of Naming the Degrees of Sound

e	la			
d	la	sol		
c	sol	fa		
b	fa	♮	mi	
a	la	mi	re	𝄞
g	sol	re	ut	
f	fa	ut		
e	la	mi		
d	la	sol	re	
c	sol	fa	ut	𝄡
b	fa	♮	mi	
a	la	mi	re	
g	sol	re	ut	
F	fa	ut		𝄢
E	la	mi		
D	sol	re		
C	fa	ut		
B	mi			
A	re			
Γ	ut			

Before we come to the tuning of these degrees, you may observe that a voice doth express a sound best when it pronounceth some word or syllable with it. For this cause, as also for order and distinction sake, six syllables were used in former times, viz. Ut, Re, Mi, Fa, Sol, La, which, being joined with the seven letters, their scale was set down in this manner.

Four of these, to wit, Mi, Fa, Sol, La (taken in their significancy), are necessary assistants to the right tuning of the degrees of sound, as will presently appear. The other two, Ut and Re, are superfluous and therefore laid aside by most modern teachers.[4]

We will therefore make use only of Mi, Fa, Sol, La, and apply them to the seven letters which stand for the degrees of sound. In order to which we must first find out where Mi is to be placed, which being known, the places of

---

[3] Simpson uses this form of treble clef throughout the book. In the examples, the treble clef, the descant clef 𝄡 the alto clef 𝄡 the tenor clef 𝄡 the baritone clef 𝄢 and the bass clef are all used.

[4] Simpson is describing the system of Fasola, practised in England during the seventeenth and eighteenth centuries. The notes c d e and f g a were sung to the syllables fa sol la; b was sung to the syllable mi, except when it was flattened. See *A Rule for placing Mi*. Various modifications of Guidonian solmization were made from about 1600 onwards, due to the increasing number of chromatic notes.

the other three are known by consequence; for Mi hath always Fa, Sol, La both above it and under it in such order and manner as you see them set in the margin. I will therefore only give you a rule for placing of Mi and the work is done.

la
sol
fa
mi
la
sol
fa

A Rule for placing Mi

The first and most natural place for Mi is in B. But if you find in that line or space which belongs to B such a little mark or letter as this (♭) which is called a ♭ flat and excludes Mi wheresoever it comes, then is Mi to be placed in E which is its second natural place. If E have also a ♭ flat in it, then of necessity you must place your Mi in A.[5]

I have seen songs with a ♭ flat standing in A, in B, and in E, all at once, by which means Mi has been extruded from all its three places,[6] but such songs are irregular, as to that which we call the Sol-fa-ing of a song, being designed for instruments rather than for voices. However, if any such song should be proposed to you, place your Mi in D with fa, sol, la above it and under it as formerly delivered.

3. Concerning ♭ Flat and ♯ Sharp

As for the   flat we last mentioned, take notice that when it is set at the beginning of a song it causes all the notes standing in that line or space to be called fa throughout the whole song. In any other place it serves only for that particular note before which it is placed. Mark also, and bear it well in mind, that wheresoever you sing fa, that fa is but the distance of a semitone or half-note from the sound of that degree which is next under it, which semitone together with its fa must of necessity come twice in every octave, the reason whereof is that the two principal concords in music, which are a fifth and an octave, would without that abatement be thrust out of their proper places. But this you will better understand hereafter.

There is yet another mark in music necessary to be known in order to the right tuning of a song which is this ♯,[7] called a sharp. This

---

[5] Mi is to be sung to the leading note. If the piece is in a minor key, mi is sung to the leading note of the relative major key. See the musical example on page 12.

[6] For example, Henry Lawes, 'More than most fair,' a setting of the eighth sonnet of Spenser's *Amoretti*. It is quoted in Bukofzer, *Music in the Baroque Era*, London, 1948, p. 185.

[7] Simpson uses the sign ✕ here, but in the examples this is modified to ✕. It occurs on all those lines and spaces where a sharp is required; for example, the key signature for D major

is if the two Fs are in constant use. Similarly occurs. When the higher chromatically altered note is used infrequently, the key signature is normal and the individual note prefixed by an accidental. The natural is not used. The sign ♭ cancels a sharp and the sign ✕ cancels a flat. The accidental ✕ as   a sharp does not apply to all notes of the same pitch throughout the bar. It is repeated when necessary within the same bar as the initial accidental. The same sign used to cancel a flat in the signature is effective for the full bar.

sharp is of a contrary nature to the ♭ flat, for whereas that ♭ flat takes away a semitone from the sound of the note before which it is set to make it more grave or flat, this ♯ doth add a semitone to his note to make it more acute or sharp.

If it be set at the beginning of a song it makes all the notes standing in that line or space to be sharp, that is, half a tone higher throughout the whole song or lesson without changing their name. In any other place it serves only for that particular note to which it is applied.

4. OF TUNING THE DEGREES OF SOUND

Tuning is no way to be taught but by tuning, and therefore you must procure some who know how to tune these degrees (which everyone doth that hath but the least skill in music) to sing them over with you until you can tune them by yourself.

If you have been accustomed to any instrument that hath frets, as viol, lute, theorbo, etc., you may by help thereof, instead of an assisting voice, guide or lead your own voice to the perfect tuning of them. For every degree is that distance of sound which is found upon any fretted instrument from the open string to the second fret, or from any one fret to the next but one to it, except that sound to which we apply fa, for fa is always but the distance of one fret from the sound of the degree next under it.

We will take the bass-viol for example in the common old tuning and in the way of tablature where six lines stand for the six strings of the viol, the highest for the highest or treble string, and so the rest in order, and letters are set for the frets, though in a different way from the scale of music, to wit (*a*) for the open string, (*b*) for the first fret, (*c*) for the second, and so the rest in order, each fret making the distance or interval of a semitone or half-note.

EXAMPLE

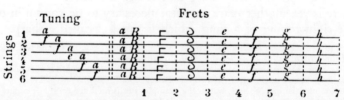

[8] The tuning refers to the relationship between the pitches of the strings, not their actual pitches. If the lowest string were tuned to G, the stopping of this string at the f fret would produce the note C, a fourth above. The fifth string would be tuned to this C. The tuning of the instrument would therefore be [notation] . The system resembles the French lute tablature, the strings being in their natural [notation] order, and the frets indicated by letters. In later editions, this passage was severely [notation] curtailed to bring the book up to date.

Our business now is to make these letters teach you to rise and fall by degrees with your voice, in case you have no other assistant. We will make use of the middle clef and take the compass of an octave, because an octave includes the chief concerns of music, and so place the letters of tablature and the degrees of sound one over the other that you may compare them, both with your eye and your ear.

EXAMPLE

Mi in B

Sol la *mi* fa sol la fa sol   Sol fa la sol fa *mi* la sol

Mi in E

Sol la fa sol la *mi* fa sol   Sol fa *mi* la sol fa la sol

Mi in A

La *mi* fa sol la fa sol la   La sol fa la sol fa *mi* la

And here you may observe what an advantage these four syllables do afford us towards the right tuning of the degrees, for, as Mi directs apt and fitting places for fa, sol and la to stand in due order both above and under it, so fa doth show us where we are to place the semitone or half-note, which, as I said, must have two places in each octave that the degrees may meet the two concords in their proper places.

Now, as you have seen the three places of Mi in the C clef, the like is to be understood of the other two clefs according to the examples following.

Mi in B

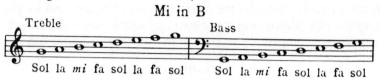

Treble   Bass

Sol la *mi* fa sol la fa sol   Sol la *mi* fa sol la fa sol

Mi in E

Treble   Bass

Sol la fa sol la *mi* fa sol   Sol la fa sol la *mi* fa sol

Mi in A

Treble   Bass

La *mi* fa sol la fa sol la   La *mi* fa sol la fa sol la

When you have brought your voice to rise and fall by degrees in manner aforesaid, I would then have you exercise it to ascend and descend by leaps to all the distances in an octave, both flat and sharp in manner as follows:

EXAMPLE

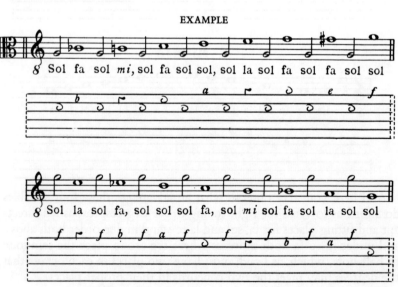

Sol fa sol *mi*, sol fa sol sol, sol la sol fa sol fa sol sol

Sol la sol fa, sol sol sol fa, sol *mi* sol fa sol la sol sol

Having spoken of naming and tuning of sounds, it now comes in order that we treat of their length or quantity, according to measure of time, which is the second concern or consideration of a sound.

5. OF NOTES, THEIR NAMES AND CHARACTERS

The first two notes in use were Nota Longa and Nota Brevis (our Long and Breve) in order to a long and short syllable. Only they doubled or trebled their Longa and called it Larga or Maxima Nota which is our Large.

When music grew to more perfection they added two notes more under the names of Semi brevis and Minima Nota (our semibreve and minim) which latter was then their shortest note.

To these, later times have added note upon note till at last we are come to Demisemiquaver, which is the shortest or swiftest note that we have now in practice. The characters and names of which notes are these that follow.

The strokes or marks which you see set after them are called Pauses[11] or Rests (that is, a cessation or intermission of sound) and are of the same length or quantity as to measure of time with the notes which stand before them, and are likewise called by the same names, as Long rest, Breve rest, Semibreve rest, etc.

And now from the names and characters of notes we will proceed to their measures, quantities and proportions.

6. OF THE ANCIENT MOODS OR MEASURES OF NOTES

In former times they had four Moods or Modes of measuring notes. The first they called Perfect of the More (Time and Prolation being implied) in which a large contained three longs, a long three breves, a breve three semibreves and a semibreve three minims. So it is set down in later authors, though I make a doubt whether semibreves

[9] The examples are written in diamond-shaped notes (with the exception of the Large, Long and Breve) as are all the examples in the second and third editions.

[10] No rest signs for semiquaver or demisemiquaver are given, but an example using semiquaver rests is shown on page 14. The sign used is simply .

[11] At this time the term *pause* did not apply to the holding of a note which had the sign ⌒ above it, but was used in the continental sense of rest. The words Pause (Ger.), Pause (Fr.) and Pausa (It.) mean a rest.

and minims (at least minims) were ever used in this Mood. Its sign was this, $\odot$3.[12]

The second Mood had the name of Perfect of the Less. In this, a large contained two longs, a long two breves, a breve three semibreves and a semibreve two minims. The time or measure-note in this Mood was the breve; the sign or mark of the Mood was this, $\bigcirc$3.[13]

The third Mood was named Imperfect of the More, in which a large contained two longs, a long two breves, a breve two semibreves and a semibreve (which was the time-note in this Mood) contained three minims. Its mark or sign was this, C3.[14]

The measure of these three Moods was Tripla, of which more hereafter. To tell you their distinction of Mood, Time and Prolation were to little purpose, the Moods themselves wherein they were concerned being now worn out of use.

The fourth Mood they named Imperfect of the Less which we now call the Common Mood, the other three being laid aside as useless. The sign of the Mood is a semicircle thus, C, sometimes with a dash or stroke through it, thus, $\mathsf{\phi}$. And this is commonly set at the beginning of songs and lessons. Though there be no sign, you may suppose this Mood because the rest are grown strangers to us. You may sometimes see this figure 3 set at the beginning of a song or lesson of which I shall speak hereafter.

In this last or common Mood, two longs make one large, two breves a long, two semibreves a breve, etc. In which order they proceed to the last or shortest note, so that a large contains two longs,

---

[12] The Great Mood refers to the number of longs in a large (three if perfect, two if imperfect), i.e. modus major or modus maximarum. The Less Mood refers to the number of breves in a long, i.e. modus minor or modus longarum, or simply modus. Similarly, Time is the number of semibreves in a breve, and Prolation, minims in a semibreve. The Great and Less Moods involved notes of such length that they were virtually theoretical, practical application of them in music defeated the abilities of the singer.

[13] Morley in his *Plain and Easy Introduction* (Harman Edition, p. 125) gives the sign of this Mood as C3 , the sign for the Great Mood Imperfect, Less Mood Imperfect, Time Perfect, Prolation Imperfect, which is what Simpson describes. (See note 14.) Playford in his *Brief Introduction to the Skill of Music* gives the sign for this Mood as C3 .

[14] Morley's sign for this Mood is C2 , the sign for Great Mood Imperfect, Less Mood Imperfect, Time Imperfect, Prolation Perfect. There is some confusion concerning these signs; both Sebald Heyden (1498–1561) in *Musicae Στοιχείωσις* (1532) and Ludovico Zacconi (1555–1627) in *Prattica di Musica* (1592), Book II, partially disagree with Morley's signs for the many Moods. (Simpson mentions only four, and his list is far from complete.) However, the signs given by Heyden and Zacconi for the second (Perfect of the Less) and third (Imperfect of the More) Moods as mentioned by Simpson, agree with the signs given by Morley. All four writers, Simpson, Morley, Heyden and Zacconi are agreed on the signs for the Moods named by Simpson as the Perfect of the More and the Imperfect of the Less. Playford gives $\frac{\phi}{3}$ or $\frac{\odot}{3}$ as signs for the Imperfect of the More but his signs agree with those given by Simpson for the Perfect of the More and the Imperfect of the Less, although he does not give C as a possible alternative to ϕ .

four breves, eight semibreves, sixteen minims, thirty-two crotchets, sixty-four quavers, etc., which for your better understanding is presented to your view in this scheme.

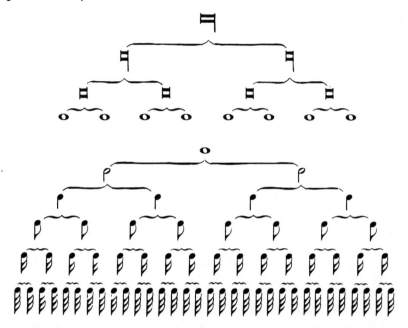

Where note that the large and long are now of little use, being too long for any voice or instrument (the organ excepted) to hold out to their full length. But their rests are still in frequent use, especially in grave music and songs of many parts.

You will say, if those notes you named be too long for the voice to hold out, to what purpose were they used formerly? To which I answer, they were used in Tripla time and in a quick measure, quicker perhaps than we now make our semibreve and minim. For as after-times added new notes, so they still put back the former into something a slower measure.

7. OF KEEPING TIME

Our next business is to consider how, in such a diversity of long and short notes, we come to give every particular note its due measure without making it either longer or shorter than it ought to be. To effect this, we use a constant motion of the hand. Or, if the hand be otherwise employed, we use the foot. If that be also engaged, the imagination (to which these are but assistant) is able of itself to perform that office. But in this place we must have recourse to the motion of the hand.

This motion of the hand is down and up, successively and equally divided, every down and up being called a time or measure,[15] and by this we measure the length of a semibreve which is therefore called the measure-note or time-note. And therefore look how many of the shorter notes go to a semibreve (as you did see in the scheme) so many do also go to every time or measure. Upon which account, two minims make a time, one down, the other up, four crotchets a time, two down and two up. Again, eight quavers a time, four down and four up. And so you may compute the rest.

But you may say, I have told you that a semibreve is the length of a time and a time the length of a semibreve, and still you are ignorant what that length is.

To which I answer, in case you have none to guide your hand at the first measuring of notes, I would have you pronounce these words—'one, two, three, four,' in an equal length as you would leisurely read them, then fancy those four words to be four crotchets which make up the quantity or length of a semibreve and consequently of a time or measure; in which, let these two words, 'one, two,' be pronounced with the hand down, and 'three, four,' with it up. In the continuation of this motion you will be able to measure and compute all your other notes. Some speak of having recourse to the motion of a lively pulse for the measure of crotchets, or to the little minutes of a steady going watch for quavers by which to compute the length of other notes, but this which I have delivered will I think be most useful to you.

It is now fit that I set you some easy and short lesson or song to exercise your hand in keeping time, to which purpose this which follows shall serve in the first place with Mi in B, according to what hath been delivered, where observe that when you see a dot[16] or point like this · , set after any note, that note must have half so much as its value comes to added to it. That is, if it be a semibreve, that semibreve with its dot must be held out the length of three minims; if it stand after a minim, that minim and the dot must be made the length of three crotchets, but still to be sung or played as one entire note. And so you may conceive of a dot after any other note.

[15] That is, a group of beats, the first accented, which may or may not be marked off by bar lines. It is possible that the word measure, meaning bar, now in common use in the U.S.A., is derived from this. Simpson distinguishes between the concept of time or measure and that of a bar. On page 11, each bar of both musical examples consists of one time or measure, but in the first example on page 93, there are presumably four times or measures to each bar. (The French for a bar is *mesure* and the Italian *misura*.)

[16] Simpson writes *prick*. This word has been altered to dot here and elsewhere. The adjectival form, *prickt*, has been changed to dotted throughout the book.

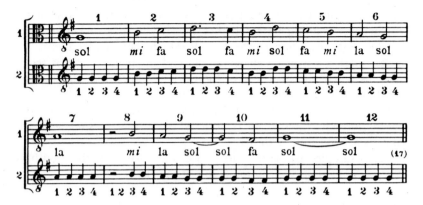

Here you have every time or measure distinguished by strokes crossing the lines, which strokes, together with the spaces betwixt them, are called Bars. In the third bar you have a minim with a dot after it, which minim and dot must be made the length of three crotchets. In the eighth bar you have a minim rest which you must silently measure as two crotchets according to the two figures you see under it.

The second staff or stanza is the same as the first, only it is broken into crotchets, four of which make a time, by which you may exactly measure the notes which stand above them according to our proposed method.

When you can sing the former example in exact time, you may try this next which hath Mi in E.

[17] Written in the alto clef in early editions. Later transposed the octave and written in the treble clef. Subsequent editions confuse many of the musical examples by using the treble clef meaning $\oint$, with curious results.

In the eighth bar of this example you have a minim rest and a crotchet rest standing both together which you may reckon as three crotchet rests according to the figures which stand under them.

This mark √ which you see at the end of the five lines is set to direct us where the first note of the next five lines doth stand and is therefore called a Director.

We will now proceed to quicker notes in which we must turn our dividing crotchets into quavers, four whereof must be sung with the hand down and four with it up.

Your example shall be set with a G clef and Mi in A, that you may be ready in naming your notes in any of the clefs.

EXAMPLE

Here you have a dotted crotchet, or crotchet with a dot after it, divided into three quavers in several places of this example, expressed by the quavers in the under staff, which quavers I would have you to sing or play often over, that they may teach you the true length of your dotted crotchet which is of very much concern for singing or playing exactly in time.

When you see an arch or stroke drawn over or under two, three or more notes like those in the lower staff of the late example, it signifies in vocal music so many notes to be sung to one syllable, as Ligatures did in former times. In music made for viols or violins, it signifies so many notes to be played with one motion of the bow.

Two strokes through the lines signify the end of a strain. If they have dots on each side thus, ⫴ , the strain is to be repeated.[19]

___

[18] See footnote 5 on p. 3.

[19] Although having dots on both sides of the double line, this sign indicates the repeat of that strain which precedes it. This sentence appears in all editions up to and including the eighth edition. In the ninth, the sentence was changed to read: 'If they have dots on each side the strains or parts *are* to be repeated.' Such signs as that given in the text occur at the end of the first section of a binary movement and occasionally at the end of the second section in which case both parts are to be repeated, e.g. No. 2 of the pieces dedicated to Sir John St. Barbe in the 'Appendix of Short and Easy Ayres.' In this example only the accompanying bass part has this repeat mark at the end of the second section. Morley also uses this sign in his *Plain and Easy Introduction*, ed. by R. A. Harman, p. 99.

This mark ⨦ signifies a repetition from that place only where it is set and is called a Repeat.[20]

This mark or arch ⌒ is commonly set at the end of a song or lesson to signify the close or conclusion. It is also set sometimes over certain particular notes in the middle of songs when, for humour, we are to insist or stay a little upon the said notes and thereupon it is called a Stay or Hold.[21]

8. OF DRIVING A NOTE

Syncope or driving a note is when after some shorter note, which begins the measure or half-measure, there immediately follow two, three or more notes of a greater quantity before you meet with another short note (like that which began the driving) to make the number even; as when an odd crotchet comes before two, three or more minims, or an odd quaver before two, three or more crotchets.[22]

To facilitate this, divide always the greater note into two of the lesser; that is, if they be minims, divide them into two crotchets apiece; if crotchets, into two quavers.

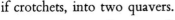

In this example the first note is a crotchet which drives through the minim in D and the measure is made even by the next crotchet in C.

The second bar begins with a dotted crotchet which is divided into three quavers in the lower staff as formerly shown. In the same bar, the crotchet in G is driven through three minims, viz. those in E, D, C, and the number is made even by the crotchet in B, which answers to that crotchet which began the driving. The fifth bar begins with a quaver which is driven through the three crotchets standing in C,

---

[20] This sign does not usually apply to complete sections as is the case with 𝄇 , but to the last few bars (e.g. No. 16 in the 'Appendix of Short and Easy Ayres') or to those pieces which consist only of one strain. However, ⨦ is placed above 𝄇 which marks the end of the first strain in the unnumbered lesson for the treble-bass viol and harpsichord in the 'Appendix.' Both sections are therefore to be repeated.

[21] Simpson does not mention that the final chord is to be prolonged when the sign is placed over it. He merely says that such a sign is used to mark the conclusion of a piece. In the fifth part of the book the sign indicates the conclusion of those notes which are to be imitated exactly by later entries in canon.

[22] This description is reminiscent of the fourteenth-century concept of syncopation. Since the tie and the bar line were unknown, it was considered that a group of notes could be split and another group of notes of larger value inserted, the rhythmic balance of the passage being righted after the longer notes by the remainder of the shorter ones. Later fourteenth-century composers (Baude Cordier, Solage, etc.) delighted in rhythmic complexities of every kind. See W. Apel, *The Notation of Polyphonic Music*, 900–1600, fourth edition, Cambridge, Mass., 1953, p. 395 ff.

B, A, and is made even by the quaver in G which answers to it and fills up the measure. All which is made easy by dividing them into such lesser notes as you see in the lower staff.

9. CONCERNING ODD RESTS

Odd rests we call those which take up only some part or parcel of a semibreve's time or measure, and have always reference to some odd note, for by these two odds the measure is made even.

Their most usual place is the beginning or middle of the time, yet sometimes they are set in the latter part of it, as it were, to fill up the measure.

If you see a short rest stand before one that is longer, you may conclude that the short rest is set there in reference to some odd note which went before. For there is no such thing as driving a shorter rest through a longer, like that which we showed in notes.

When two minim rests stand together in common time, you may suppose that the first of them belongs to the foregoing time and the second to the time following, otherwise they would have been made one entire semibreve rest.[23]

When we have a minim rest with a crotchet rest after it, we commonly count them as three crotchet rests. In like manner we reckon a crotchet and a quaver rest as three quaver rests, and a quaver and semiquaver as three semiquaver rests.

Concerning the minim and crotchet rest I need say no more, supposing you are already well enough informed in their measure by what has been delivered. The chief difficulty is in the other two, to wit, the quaver and the semiquaver rests which indeed are most concerned in instrumental music.

Your best way to deal with these at first is to play them as you would do notes of the same quantity, placing those supposed or feigned notes in such places as you think most convenient. I will give you one example which being well considered and practised will do the business.

[23] Simpson distinguishes between *time* or *measure* and bar. (See footnote 15 on p. 10). There must be two or more *times* in one bar for two minim rests to occur.

Practice this example, first according to the second or lower staff. And when you have made that perfect, leave out the notes which have crosses over them, together with the bows which did express them, and then it will be the same as the first staff. By this means you will get a true habit of making these short rests in their due measure.

The notes you see with one dash or stroke through their tails are quavers. Those with two strokes are semiquavers. When they have three or four strokes, they are demisemiquavers.

10. OF TRIPLA TIME

When you see this figure 3 set at the beginning of a song or lesson, it signifies that the time or measure must be counted by threes, as we formerly did it by fours.

Sometimes the Tripla consists of three semibreves to a measure, each semibreve being shorter than a minim in common time.

The measure of this Tripla is like the Mood we formerly mentioned called Perfect of the Less, in which three semibreves went to a measure.

The more common Tripla is three minims to a measure, each minim about the length of a crotchet in common time, and this Tripla is the same as the Mood Imperfect of the More as to measure of time, only we count but two minims to a semibreve, which in that Mood contained three.

In these two sorts of Tripla we count or imagine these two words, 'one, two,' with the hand down, and this word, 'three,' with it up. I will set down their examples in the bass clef because hitherto we have made no use of it.

Tripla of 3 semibreves to a measure[24]

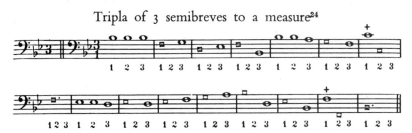

When the shorter note comes before the longer in the same time or measure, as in two places of this last example, marked with little crosses, it is usual with some to make them both black, in this manner.

[24] In later editions this example was written in '3 minims to a measure' and the note values of other examples halved in order to modernize the book.

The like they do also in Triplas of three minims when the minim comes before the semibreve, thus:

which I suppose they do only to show that the short note belongs to that which follows, not to that which went before, seeing they do not intend thereby any diminution of their value, which blacking of notes doth properly signify as will be shown hereafter.[25]

Tripla of Three Minims to a Measure

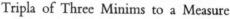

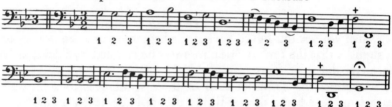

There are divers Triplas of a shorter measure which by reason of their quick movement are usually measured by counting three down and three up with the hand so that of them it may be said that two measures make but one time. And those quick Triplas are dotted sometimes with minims and crotchets and sometimes with black semibreves instead of minims, and black minims which in appearance are crotchets. I will set you one example written both ways that you may not be ignorant of either when they shall be laid before you.

Tripla of Three Crotchets to a Measure

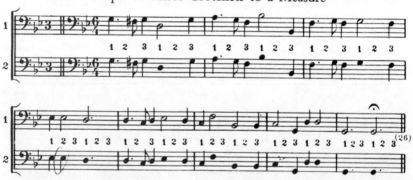

[25] These notes do not appear to have a connection with coloration as used in the mensural notation in the fifteenth and sixteenth centuries. Three black notes, equal to two white notes, sometime resulted in a change of accent, as from $\frac{6}{8}$ time to $\frac{3}{4}$ time; e.g. The use of the blackened breve and the blackened semibreve in the text does show a similar shift of accent from the third to the second beat of the bar, but in later examples, these blackened notes are used when no shift of accent is apparent.

[26] The black semibreve ceased to be used about 1700: the teaching of the use of this type of notation does not appear in the fourth edition of Simpson's book dated 1706.

Take notice that the black semibreves as also the minims which stand over them are sung or played as fast in these quick Triplas as crotchets in common time, and the black minims or crotchets, call them which you please, as fast as quavers. The like consideration may be had of the former Triplas as well of three semibreves as three minims to a measure, for in all Triplas the notes are sung or played much quicker than they are in common time.

Beside these several sorts of Triplas before mentioned, you may sometimes meet with figures set thus, $\frac{3}{2}$ called Sesquialtera proportion[27] which signifies a Tripla measure of three notes to two suchlike notes of the common time. The like may be understood of $\frac{6}{4}$ or any other proportion, which proportions, if they be of the greater inequality, that is when the greater figure doth stand above, do always signify diminution, of which I will speak a little in this place.

II. OF DIMINUTION

Diminution, in this acceptation, is the lessening or abating something of the full value or quantity of notes, a thing much used in former times when the Tripla Moods were in fashion. Their first sorts of diminution were by note, by rest and by colour. By note, as when a semibreve followed a breve, in the Mood Perfect of the Less, that breve was to be made but two semibreves, which otherwise contained three.[28] The like was observed if a minim came after a semibreve in the Mood named Imperfect of the More, in which a semibreve contained three minims.

By rest, as when such rests were set after like notes.[29]

By colour, as when any of the greater notes which contained three of the lesser were made black, by which they were diminished a third part of their value.[30]

Another sign of diminution is the turning of the sign of the Mood backward thus, $\supset$, being still in use, which requires each note to be

[27] Proportio sesquialtera: in mensural notation, the placing of the sign $\frac{3}{2}$ indicated that the notes in the following passage were to have two-thirds of their previous value. Thus three notes were to be sung in the time of two, e.g. ♢ ♢ $\frac{3}{2}$ ♢♢♢ = ♩ ♩ |♩♩♩|

[28] See page 8. In Mood Perfect of the Less, Time was perfect and the breve divided into three semibreves. By the principles of imperfection or alteration the breve could be reduced to the value of two semibreves and similarly the value of the semibreve could be doubled. If a breve were followed by one, or by more than three semibreves, it assumed the value of two semibreves, thus being reduced from its normal value of three semibreves.

[29] A rest could not be imperfected (altered in value) but its position could result in the note preceding or the note following being altered. A breve followed by a semibreve rest was equal to two semibreves. A semibreve following a semibreve rest was equal to two semibreves.

[30] The breve, the semibreve and the minim could be blackened and the normal acceptation was that three of these blackened notes were equal to two of their white equivalents.

played or sung twice so quick as when it stands the usual way.[31] Also a dash or stroke through the sign of the Mood, thus ₵, is properly a sign of diminution, though many dash it so without any such intention.

They had yet more signs of diminution as crossing or double-dashing the sign of the Mood, also the setting of figures to signify diminution in dupla, tripla and quadrupla proportion, with other such-like, which being now out of use, I will trouble you no further with them. And this is as much as I thought necessary for tuning and timing of notes which is all that belongs to the Rudiments of Song.

---

[31] A line drawn through the mensuration sign ₵ , ₵ , indicated proportio dupla and the reducing of the note values by half their original length, just as the sign $\frac{3}{2}$ indicated proportio sesquialtera. See footnote 27 on p. 17.

THE SECOND PART

TEACHING THE PRINCIPLES OF COMPOSITION

1. Of Counterpoint

BEFORE notes of different measure were in use, their way of composing was to set dots or points one against another to denote the concords, the length or measure of which points was sung according to the quantity of the words or syllables which were applied to them. And because in composing our descant we set note against note, as they did point against point, from thence it still retains the name of Counterpoint.[1]

In reference to composition in counterpoint I must propose unto you the bass as the groundwork or foundation upon which all musical composition is to be erected, and from this bass we are to measure or compute all those distances or intervals which are requisite for the joining of other parts thereto.[2]

2. Of Intervals[3]

An interval in music is that distance or difference which is betwixt any two sounds where the one is more grave, the other more acute.

In reference to intervals we are first to consider a unison, that is, one or the same sound whether produced by one single voice or divers voices sounding in the same tone.

This unison, as it is the first term to any interval, so may it be considered in music as a unit in arithmetic or as a point in geometry, not divisible.

As sounds are more or less distant from any supposed unison, so do they make greater or lesser intervals, upon which account, intervals may be said to be like numbers, indefinite. But those which we are here to consider be only such as are contained within our common scale of music, which may be divided into so many particles or sections

---

[1] From the Latin punctus contra punctum and therefore note against note which, in Simpson's examples, resemble chords rather than moving lines. (See Introduction, p. xxv.) The examples appear to be homophonic but Simpson adds one part at a time in his teaching method, suggesting a contrapuntal approach. Although not primarily concerned with the relationship of the upper parts to each other, Simpson is most careful about the relationship of these parts to the bass. The bass part is written with the emphasis on harmonic rather than melodic concept.

[2] See Introduction, p. xxv.

[3] Chapters 2–5 are similar in content and treatment to material to be found in Simpson's book, The Division-Viol, Part II. (See Introduction, pp. xxxv–xxxvi, and footnote 14 on p. 24 and footnote 1 on p. 40.)

only as there be semitones or half-notes contained in the said scale: that is to say, twelve in every octave as may be observed in the stops of fretted instruments[4] or in the keys of a common harpsichord or organ. Their names are these that follow:

12. Diapason[5]	12. Octave, or 8ve[6]
11. Semidiapason	11. Defective 8ve
11. Sept. major	11. Greater 7th
10. Sept. minor	10. Lesser 7th
9. Hexachordon ma.	9. Greater 6th
8. Hexachordon mi.	8. Lesser 6th
7. Diapente	7. Perfect 5th
6. Semidiapente	6. Imperfect 5th
6. Tritone	6. Greater 4th
5. Diatessaron	5. Perfect 4th
4. Ditone	4. Greater 3rd
3. Semiditone·	3. Lesser 3rd
2. Tone	2. Greater 2nd
1. Semitone	1. Lesser 2nd
Unison	One sound

Where take notice that the defective 8ve and greater 7th are the same interval in the scale of music. The like may be said of the defective 5th and greater 4th. Also you may observe that the particle Semi in Semidiapason, Semidiapente, etc., doth not signify the half of such an interval in music, but only imports a deficiency as wanting a semitone of perfection.

Out of these semitones or half-notes arise all those intervals or distances which we call concords and discords.

3. OF CONCORDS

Concords in music are these, 3rd, 5th, 6th, 8ve. By which I also mean their octaves, as 10th, 12th, 13th, 15th, etc. All other intervals

---

[4] The frets on European instruments always divide the fingerboard in such a way as to produce a semitone from each division.

[5] The mediaeval names of the intervals, taken from the Greek and Latin with certain modifications.

[6] Simpson refers to 8*ths* throughout the book. This has been changed to 8ves.

as 2nd, 4th, 7th, and their octaves, reckoning from the bass are discords, as you see in the following scale.

Concords	Concords	Discords
8 O 22		
5 O 19	6 O 20	7 O 21
	3 O 17	4 O 18
8 O 15		2 O 16
		7 O 14
5 O 12	6 O 13	
	3 O 10	4 O 11
		2 O 9
8 O		7 O
5 O	6 O	
	3 O	4 O
		2 O
O	O	O
Perfect	**Imperfect**	**Discords**

As you see the concords and discords computed here from the lowest line upward, so are they to be reckoned from any line or space wherein any note of the bass doth stand.

Again, concords are of two sorts, perfect and imperfect, as you see denoted under the scale. Perfects are these, 5th, 8ve, with all their octaves. Imperfects are a 3rd, 6th, and their octaves as you see in the scale.

Imperfects have yet another distinction, to wit, the greater and lesser 3rd, as also the greater and lesser 6th.

4. PASSAGE OF THE CONCORDS

First take notice that perfects of the same kind as two 5ths or two 8ves rising or falling together are not allowed in composition, as thus:

Not allowed   Not allowed

5   5   5   5   8   8   8   8   (7)

But if the notes do either keep still in the same line or space, or remove upward or downward into the octave, two, three, or more perfects of the same kind may in that way be allowed.

EXAMPLE
Allowed   Allowed

5   5   5   5   5   5   5   8   8   8   8   8   8   8

---

[7] Simpson gives an example by Kapsperger on page 68 which has four 5ths in succession and qualifies his opinion.

Also in composition of many parts, where necessity so requires, two 5ths or two 8ves may be tolerated, the parts passing in contrary motion, thus:

Allowed in composition of many parts

The passage from a 5th to an 8ve or from an 8ve to a 5th is, for the most part, allowable, so that the upper part remove but one degree.

As for 3rds or 6ths which are imperfect concords, two, three or more of them ascending or descending together are allowable and very usual.

In fine, you have liberty to change from any one to any other different concord, some few passages excepted as being less elegant in composition of two or three parts, though in more parts more allowance may be granted to them. The passages are these that follow.[9]

Passages not allowed in few parts

The reason why these passages are not allowed shall be shown hereafter.[10]

5. Concerning the Key or Tone

Every composition of music, be it long or short, is (or ought to be) designed to some one key or tone in which the bass doth always

---

[8] See musical example on page 38. In the following sentence, the words 'so that the upper part remove but one degree' are not in the second edition.

[9] In the 3rd edition the first part of this paragraph reads: 'In fine you have liberty to change from any one to any other different concord. First, when one of the parts keeps its place; secondly, when both the parts remove together, some few passages excepted, as being. . . .'

[10] See Chapter 6 of Part IV. This sentence is not in the second edition.

conclude. This key is said to be either Flat or Sharp,[11] not in respect
of itself, but in relation to the flat or sharp 3rd which is joined to it.

To distinguish this you are first to consider its 5th which consists
always of a lesser and a greater 3rd, as you see in these two instances,
the key being in G.

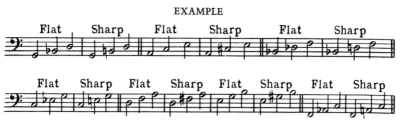

If the lesser 3rd be in the lower place next to the key, then is the
music said to be set in a flat key. But if the greater 3rd stand next to
the key as it doth in the second instance, then the key is called sharp.

I will show you this flat and sharp 3rd applied to the key in all the
usual places of an octave, to which may be referred such as are less
usual, for however the key be placed, it must always have its 5th
divided according to one of these two ways, and consequently must
be either a flat or a sharp key.

EXAMPLE

As the bass is set in a flat or a sharp key, so must the other parts be
set with flats or sharps in all the octaves above it.

6. OF THE CLOSES OR CADENCES BELONGING TO THE KEY

Having spoken of the key or tone, it follows in order that we speak
of the closes or cadences which belong unto it. And here we must
have recourse to our forementioned 5th and its two 3rds, for upon
them depends the air of every composition, they serving as bounds
or limits which keep the music in a due decorum.

True it is that a skilful composer may for variety carry on his music
sometimes to make a middle close or cadence in any key, but here we
are to instruct a beginner and to show him what closes or cadences
are most proper and natural to the key in which a song is set.

Of these, the chief and principal is the key itself in which, as hath
been said, the bass must always conclude, and this may be used also
for a middle close near the beginning of a song, if one think fit. The
next in dignity[12] is the 5th above and the next after that, the 3rd. In

[11] = minor or major.   [12] = In importance.

these three places, middle closes may properly be made when the key is flat.

EXAMPLE

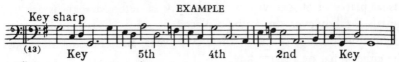

Key flat

Key   5th   3rd   Key

But if the bass be set in a sharp key, then it is not so proper nor easy to make a middle close or cadence to end upon the sharp 3rd and therefore (instead thereof) we commonly make use of the 4th or 2nd above the key for middle closes.

EXAMPLE

Key sharp

(13)   Key   5th   4th   2nd   Key

Thus you see what closes belong to the key, both flat and sharp, and by these two examples set in G you may know what is to be done, though the key be removed to any other letter of the scale.

7. How to Frame a Bass[14]

1. Let the air[15] of your bass be proper to the key designed.

2. If it have middle closes, let them be according to the late examples.

3. The longer your bass is, the more middle closes will be required.

4. The movement of your bass must be for the most part by leaps of a 3rd, 4th or 5th, using degrees no more than to keep it within the proper bounds and air of the key. Lastly, I would have you to make choice of a flat key to begin with and avoid the setting of sharp notes in the bass for some reasons which shall appear hereafter. Let this short bass which follows serve for an instance, in which there is a close or section at the end of the second bar.

EXAMPLE

♭ Bass

[13] This example is lacking a sharp in the signature, but since the f is natural both times it appears on account of the suggested modulation, there is no need of it. The use of sharp key signatures did not appear until the middle of the seventeenth century and those key signatures then used are frequently misleading. Flat keys usually had a signature of one flat less than those of to-day; sharp keys had one sharp less, the leading note being sharpened by an accidental when necessary.

[14] Chapters 7–10 are similar in content and treatment to material to be found in Simpson's book, *The Division-Viol*, Part II. (See Introduction, pp. xxxv and xxxvi, and footnote 3 on p. 19 and footnote 1 on p. 40.)

[15] Simpson writes aire. Most seventeenth-century writers use the term aire (ayre) to mean key or mode. Morley writes: 'The perfect knowledge of these airs (which the antiquity termed Modi) was in such estimation . . .,' p. 249 of the *Plain and Easy Introduction* (Harman edition). Also Butler, *The Principles of Musick*, 1636, p. 80; Mace, *Musick's Monument*, 1676, p. 104; all use the term in this connection. Simpson is using the term as Purcell did, to mean melodic line. See Introduction, p. xxii, and footnote 24 on p. 75. The word is also used on pp. 70, 71, 73, 75 and 78.

8. How to Join a Treble to the Bass[16]

The bass being made, your next business is to join a treble to it, which to effect (after you have placed your treble clef) you are to set a note of the same quantity with the first note of your bass, either in a 3rd, 5th or 8ve above your bass, for we seldom begin with a 6th in counterpoint.

Now for carrying on the rest, your securest way is to take that concord, note after note, which may be had with the least remove, and that will be either by keeping in the same place or removing but one degree. In this manner you may proceed until you come to some close or section of the strain, at which you may remove by leap to what concord you please and then carry on the rest as before.

By this means you will be less liable to those disallowances formerly mentioned, most of them being occasioned by leaps of the upper part.

Only let me advise[17] you that we seldom use 8ves in two parts except beginning notes, ending notes or where the parts move contrary, that is one rising, the other falling.

If you set a figure under each note as you write[18] it to signify what concord it is to the bass, as you see in the following examples, it will be some ease to your eye and memory.

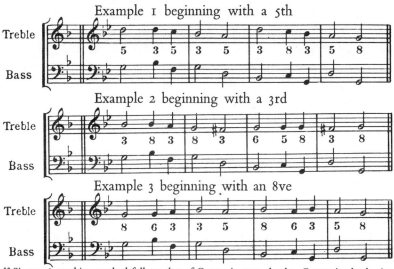

[16] Simpson's teaching method follows that of Coperario very closely. Coperario also begins with the movement of the bass and then adds his treble to it. The other parts must then have those notes which remain. *Rules how to Compose*, ed. by Manfred F. Bukofzer, Los Angeles, 1952.

[17] Simpson writes: 'Only let me advertise you. . . .' The word is used again on p. 93, and in both cases has been changed to advise.

[18] Simpson uses the word *prick*. This has been changed to *write* here and elsewhere. Similarly the word *prickt* as used by Simpson has been replaced by *written*. Occasionally the words *prick down* or *prickt down* occur in Simpson's text and these have been altered to *set down*. The word *prick* is also used by Simpson to mean *dot*. See footnote 16 on p. 10. The words 'provided those leaps be made into imperfect concords' on p. 26 are not in the second edition.

Take notice that the bass, making a middle close at the end of the second bar, your treble may properly remove by leap at that place to any other concord and then begin a new movement by degrees, as you see in the first example.

I propose this movement by degrees as the most easy and most natural to the treble part in plain counterpoint, yet I do not so confine you thereto, but that you may use leaps when there shall be any occasion or when your own fancy shall move you thereto, provided those leaps be made into imperfect concords, as you may see by this example.

Having told you that we seldom use 8ves in two parts, 'tis fit I give you some account of those in the late examples. The first is in the third bar of the first example, where the treble meets the bass in contrary motion, therefore allowable. In the second example are three 8ves; the first in the first bar, the treble keeping its place and therefore allowable, in my opinion. The second meets in contrary motion, the third keeps its place. In the third example are two 8ves, the first begins the strain, the second the latter part thereof, in all which beginnings an 8ve may properly be used. Lastly, all those 8ves which you see at the conclusion of the examples are not only allowable but most proper and natural.

As for those two sharps which you see in the second example, the first of them is disputable as many times it happens in music, in which doubts the ear is always to be umpire.[19] The other sharp depends more upon a rule, which is that when the bass doth fall a 5th or rise a 4th, that note from which it so rises or falls doth commonly require the sharp or greater 3rd to be joined to it. And being here at the conclusion, it hath a further concern which is, that a binding cadence[20] is made of that greater 3rd by joining part of it to the foregoing note, which is as frequent in music at the close or conclusion as Amen at the end of a prayer. Examples of it are these that follow.

[19] This wavering between the use of the flattened or sharpened leading note shows a feeling for modality. It is interesting to observe that the sharpened leading note was more commonly used in the fourteenth century than the sixteenth century.
[20] That is, a cadence which is preceded by a suspension.

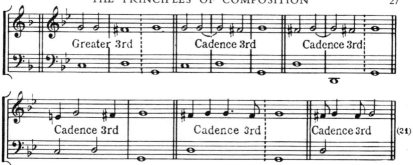

This cadence may be used by any part which hath the greater 3rd in the next note before a close.

There is another sort of cadence frequent in music (but not at conclusion) in which the greater 6th doth lend part of its note to the note which went before, the bass descending a tone or semitone, thus:

This also is appliable by any part or in any key where the greater 6th is joined to such notes of the bass.

. I would now have you frame a bass of your own according to former instructions and try how many several ways you can make a treble to it.

When you find yourself perfect and ready therein, you may try how you can add an inner part to your treble and bass, concerning which, take these instructions.

9. Composition of Three Parts

First you are to set the notes of this part in concords different from those of the treble. 2. When the treble is a 5th to the bass I would

[21] The sixteenth-century 4–3 suspension cadence. It is odd that Simpson does not give examples of the Plagal cadence which appeared about 1450. The use of the anticipation of the tonic note in the penultimate chord which was so popular in the seventeenth century is not mentioned.

[22] An adaptation of the old cadence (pre 1450) using II to I in the lowest part which stems from the Landini cadence where the 6th degree is placed between the leading note and the tonic, usually accompanied by the sharpended 4th. A Landini cadence using the above notes would be:

It eventually became the Phrygian cadence.

have you make use either of a 3rd or an 8ve for the other part and not to use a 6th therewith until I have shown you how and where a 5th and 6th may be joined together, of which more hereafter.[23]   3. You are to avoid 8ves in this inner part likewise, so much as you can with convenience. For though we use 5ths as much as imperfects, yet we seldom make use of 8ves in three parts unless in such places as we formerly mentioned. The reason why we avoid 8ves in two or three parts is that imperfect concords afford more variety upon account of their majors and minors; besides, imperfects do not cloy the ear so much as perfects do.

We will make use of the former examples that you may perceive thereby how another part is to be added.[24]

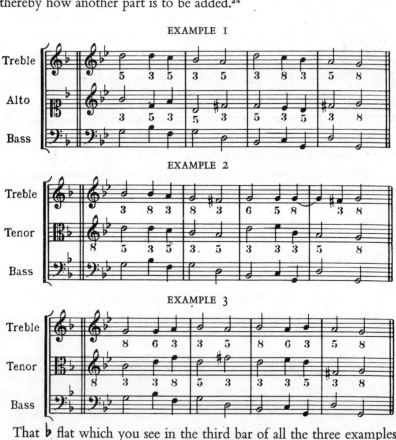

That ♭ flat which you see in the third bar of all the three examples of the inner part is set there to take away the harsh reflection of E

---

[23] See Chapter 11 of Part II.
[24] The former examples are those in two parts on p. 25, but a 4-3 suspension is added in the last bar of example 2.

natural[25] against B flat, the foregoing note of the bass, which is that we call Relation Inharmonical of which I shall speak hereafter.[26] As for the sharps, I refer you to what I said formerly of them. Only take notice that part of the sharp 3rd in the treble part of the second example is joined to the foregoing note to make that binding cadence we formerly mentioned.

10. Composition of Four Parts

If you design your composition for four parts, I would then have you join your alto as near as you can to the treble, which is easily done by taking those concords (note after note) which are next under the treble in manner as follows:

EXAMPLE

I make the alto and treble end both in the same tone which, in my opinion, is better than to have the treble end in the sharp 3rd above, the key of the composition being flat, and the sharp 3rd more proper for an inner part at conclusion.

I will now by adding another part (viz. a tenor) show you the accomplishment of four parts, concerning which these rules are to be observed.

First, that this part which is to be added be set in concords different from the other two upper parts. That is to say, if those be a 5th and 3rd, let this be an 8ve, by which you may conceive the rest.

Secondly I would have you join this tenor as near the alto as the different concords do permit, for the harmony is better when the three upper parts are joined close together.

Thirdly you are to avoid two 8ves or two 5ths rising or falling

[25] Simpson writes *E sharp*. As there was no sign for a natural at this time, the word *flat* was sometimes used to mean a natural cancelling a sharp and the word *sharp* was sometimes used to mean a natural cancelling a flat in addition to their normal meanings. E was thus either sharp or flat; so was B, the word *sharp* in both these cases meaning natural. F could be either sharp or flat also, but in this case the word *flat* meant natural. (See also footnote 7 on p. 3.) I have distinguished between these meanings throughout the book and replaced the words *flat* and *sharp* by the word *natural* when this is what is meant. The use of the E flat in the tenor part in the third bar of each of these examples avoids the tritone which would be produced by cross relation. It is employed according to the rules of musica ficta.

[26] See Chapter 7 of Part III.

together, as well amongst the upper parts as betwixt any one part and the bass, of which there is less danger by placing the parts in different concords.

Example of Four Parts

Here you may perceive each note of the newly added tenor set in a concord still different from those of the other two higher parts, by which the composition is completed in four parts. And though I have shown this composition by adding one part after another which I did conceive to be the easiest way of giving you a clear understanding of it, yet now that you know how to place the concords, it is left to your liberty to carry on your parts (so many as you design) together, and to dispose them into several concords as you shall think convenient.

11. How a 5th and 6th may stand together in Counterpoint[28]

It is generally delivered by most authors which I have seen that how many parts soever a composition consists of, there can be but three several concords joined at once to any one note of the bass; that is to say either a 3rd, 5th and 8ve, or a 3rd, 6th and 8ve, and that when the 5th takes place, the 6th is to be omitted, and contrarily if the 6th be used, the 5th is to be left out.

Our excellent and worthy countryman Mr. Morley, in his *Introduction to Music*, page 143,[29] teaching his scholar to compose four parts, useth these words: 'But when you put in a 6th, then of force

---

[27] In the eighth edition, the four parts in order are: 1st treble, 2nd treble, tenor and bass. The change of the name of this part from *alto* to *2nd treble* is perhaps due to the original clef written by Simpson. It is the soprano or descant clef, not the alto clef.

[28] A discussion of the first inversion of the seventh chord.

[29] Morley, *op. cit.* (ed. by R. A. Harman), p. 243. The example in semibreves is also taken from the same page of Morley's book and copied with the suspended D in the tenor part falling on to a strong beat.

must the 5th be left out, except at a cadence or close where a discord is taken thus:

which is the best manner of closing and the only way of taking a 5th and 6th together.'

All this is to be understood as speaking of a perfect 5th. But there is another 5th in music called a false, defective or imperfect 5th which necessarily requires a 6th to be joined with it. And though I never heard any approved author account it for a concord, yet it is of most excellent use in composition, and hath a particular grace and elegancy even in this plain way of counterpoint. It is commonly produced by making the lower term or bass note sharp as you see in these two instances.

Thus you see how a 5th and 6th may be used at once; in any other way than these I have mentioned, I do not conceive how they can stand together in counterpoint; but when one of them is put in, the other is to be left out according to the common rule.

12. Composition in a sharp Key

We will now proceed to a sharp key in which 6ths are very frequent for there are certain sharp notes of the bass which necessarily require a lesser 6th to be joined to them. As namely:

1. The half note or lesser 2nd under the key of the composition.
2. The greater 3rd above the key.

3. Also the 3rd under it, requiring sometimes the greater and sometimes the lesser 6th to be joined to it, as you see in the subsequent example in which the notes of the bass requiring a 6th are marked with little crosses under them.

Things to be noted in this example are these:

1. When the notes of the bass keep still in the same place, it is left to your liberty to remove the other parts as you shall think fit, an instance whereof you have in the next notes after the beginning.

2. Take notice and observe it hereafter that the half note or sharp second under the key doth hardly admit an 8ve to be joined to it without offence to a critical ear[30] and therefore have I joined two 6ths and a 3rd to that sharp note of the bass in F.

3. In the first part of the second bar you may see the treble lending part of its 6th to the foregoing note to make that binding cadence which we formerly mentioned, page 26.

4. You may observe that now I permit the treble to end in a sharp 3rd which I did not approve when the key was flat.[31]

The figures show you which parts are 6ths to the bass, as the marks [show you] which notes of the bass require them; where you must know that the bass in all suchlike notes doth assume the nature of an upper part, wanting commonly a 3rd, sometimes a 5th of that latitude or compass which is proper to the true nature of a bass.

To demonstrate this we will remove the said notes into their proper compass and then you will see those 6ths changed into other concords, the upper parts remaining the same they were or else using those notes which the bass assumed before.

---

[30] Doubling the leading note.   [31] See p. 29.

EXAMPLE

Treble
Alto
Tenor
Bass

Here you may perceive that by removing those notes of the bass a 3rd lower, all the 6ths are taken away except that 6th which made the binding cadence, and that also will be taken quite away if we remove its bass note into its full latitude which is a 5th lower, as you will easily see by the instance next following.

By this which hath been shown, you see where 6ths are to be used in composition and how they may be avoided when you please. But I would have you take notice that basses consisting much of notes which require 6ths to be joined to them are more apt for few than for many parts.[32]

13. Of Transition or Breaking a Note[33]

One thing yet remains, very necessary sometimes in composition, and that is to make smooth or sweeten the roughness of a leap by a gradual transition to the note next following which is commonly called the breaking of a note. The manner of it you have in the following examples where the minim in B is broken to a 3rd, 4th and 5th, both downward and upward.

---

[32] The examples in 5, 6, 7 and 8 parts on pp. 35, 36 and 38 contain only one first inversion chord. In the third edition a sentence is added at the end of this paragraph: 'The like may be said of basses that move much by degrees.'   [33] The use of passing notes.

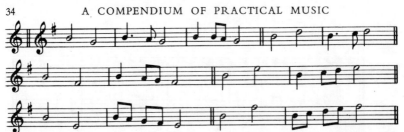

In like manner may a semibreve be broken into smaller notes. Where take notice also that two, three, or more notes standing together in the same line or space may be considered as one entire note and consequently capable of transition.

EXAMPLE

In which you have no more to take care of but that the first particle express the concord and that the last produce not two 5ths or 8ves with some other part. To avoid which, if it so happen, the following note of the other part may be altered or the transition may be omitted.

We will take the late example with its 6ths and apply some of these breakings to such notes as do require them or may admit them.

EXAMPLE

The breakings are marked with little stars under them which you will better conceive if you cast your eye back upon their original notes.

In this I have made the treble and alto end both in the same tone that you might see the tenor fall by transition into the greater 3rd at the close.

These rules and instructions which I have now delivered being duly observed may (I doubt not) suffice to show you what is necessary for composition of two, three or four parts in counterpoint.

I have set my examples all in the same key (viz. in G) that I might give the less disturbance to your apprehension; which being once confirmed, you may set your compositions in what key you please, having regard to the greater and lesser 3rd as hath been shown.

14. COMPOSITION OF 5, 6 AND 7 PARTS

By that which hath been shown, it plainly appears that there can be but three different concords applied at once to any one note of the bass, that is to say (generally speaking) either a 3rd, 5th and 8ve, or a 3rd, 6th and 8ve. Hence it follows that if we join more parts than three to the bass, it must be done by doubling some of those concords, v.g.[34] if one part more be added, which makes a composition of five parts, some one of the said concords must still be doubled. If two be added, which makes a composition of six parts, the duplication of two of the concords will be required. If three parts more be added, which makes up seven parts, then all the three concords will be doubled. And consequently the more parts a composition consists of, the more redoublings of the concords will be required. Which redoublings must be either in their octaves or in their unisons. I mention unisons because many parts cannot stand within the compass of the scale of music, but some of those parts must of necessity meet sometimes in unison.

That I may explain these things more clearly I will set you examples of 5, 6 and 7 parts, with such observations as may occur therein. And being able to join so many parts together in counter point, you will find less difficulty to compose them in figurate descant because in that you will have more liberty to change or break off upon the middle of a note.

Examples of Five Parts

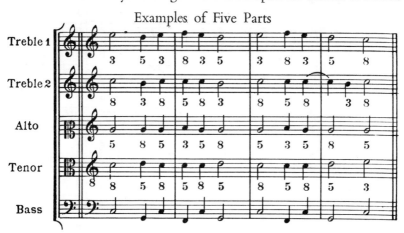

Here you see some one of the concords still doubled as may be observed by the figures which denote them. Your next shall be of six parts wherein two concords will still be doubled to each note of the bass.

[34] Verbi gratiâ—for example.

Examples of Six Parts

Here you see two concords doubled in which all you have to observe is how they remove several ways, one upward, the other downward, by which means they avoid the consecution of perfects of the same kind.

Example of Seven Parts

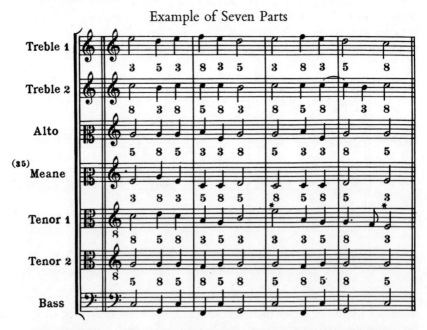

---

[35] The middle part. In fourteenth-century Fauxbourdon style in three parts, the middle voice was called the *meane*. Why it should be used in this 7 part example and not in the earlier 5 or 3 part examples is not clear. Simpson refers to the *alto* as *alt* throughout the book.

Observations in this example are these; first that all the three concords are either doubled, or if any one stand single (as that which makes the binding cadence must always do) it doth necessitate some other concord to be trebled. Secondly, that though the parts do meet sometimes in unison when it cannot be avoided, yet they must not remain so longer than necessity requires. Lastly take notice that the notes of one part may be placed above or below the notes of another neighbouring part, either to avoid the consecution of perfects or upon any voluntary design. The notes so transposed are marked with little stars over them that you may take notice of them.

15. OF TWO BASSES AND COMPOSITION OF EIGHT PARTS

Many compositions are said to have two basses (because they are exhibited by two viols or voices) when in reality they are both but one bass divided into several parcels, of which either bass doth take its part by turns whilst the other supplies the office of an upper part. Such are commonly designed for instruments. But here we are to speak of two basses of a different nature and that in reference to composition of eight parts, which, whether intended for church or chamber, is usually parted into two choirs, either choir having its peculiar bass with three upper parts thereto belonging.

These two choirs answer each other by turns, sometimes with a single voice, sometimes with two, three or all four, more or less according to the subject, matter or fancy of the composer. But when both choirs join together, the composition consists of eight parts according to the following example, in which you will see two basses, either of them moving according to the nature of that part and either of them also, if set alone, a true bass to all the upper parts of either choir; for such ought the two basses to be which here I do mean. And though it be a thing which few of our chief composers do observe, yet I cannot but deliver my opinion therein, leaving the skilful to follow which way they most affect.

Example of Eight Parts

As concerning the concordance of these two basses betwixt them-selves, it must be in every respective note either an octave, a unison, a third or a sixth, one to the other; not a fifth because the upper bass, being set alone or sounding louder than the other, will be a 4th to all those upper parts which were octaves to the lower bass. But where the basses are a 3rd one to the other, if you take away the lower bass, the 8ves are only changed into 6ths. Again, if you take away the lower bass where they are a 6th one to the other, those upper parts which were 6ths to the lower bass will be 8ves to the higher. Where the basses sound in unison or octave, the upper concords are the same to either.

The reason why I do not affect a 5th betwixt the two basses in choral music is that I would not have the music of one choir to depend upon the bass of the other which is distant from it, but rather that the music of either choir be built upon its own proper bass, and those two basses with all their upper parts to be such as may make one entire harmony when they join together.

One thing more concerning two basses is that though they may often meet in 3rds, yet if they move successively in simple 3rds, they will produce a kind of buzzing in low notes especially (as I have sometimes observed) which is not to be approved unless the humour of the words should require it.

What we have said of four parts in a choir, the same may be understood if either choir consist of five or six voices. Also if the music be composed for three or four choirs, each choir ought to have its peculiar bass, independent of the other; and the more parts the composition consists of when all are joined together in a full chorus, the greater allowances may be granted, because the multiplicity of voices doth drown or hide those little solecismes which in fewer parts would not be allowed.

This is as much as I think necessary to be shown concerning counterpoint or plain descant which is the groundwork, or (as I may say) the grammar of musical composition. And though the examples herein set down, in which I have endeavoured no curiosity but plain instruction, be short, suitable to a Compendium, yet they are, I hope, sufficient to let you see how to carry on your compositions to what length you shall desire.

THE THIRD PART

TEACHING THE USE OF DISCORDS

1. Concerning Discords

Discords as we formerly said of intervals are indefinite, for all intervals excepting those few which precisely terminate the concords are discords. But our concern in this place is no more than with these that follow, viz. the lesser and greater second, the lesser, greater and perfect fourth, the lesser or defective fifth, the lesser and greater seventh. By these I also mean their octaves.

2. How Discords are admitted into Music[1]

Discords are two ways chiefly used in composition. First, in diminution; that is, when two, three or more notes of one part are set against one note of a different part. And this is commonly done in making a gradual transition from one concord to another of which you had some intimation, page 33, where I spoke of breaking a note.

In this way of passage a discord may be allowed in any one of the diminute notes, except the first or leading note[2] which ought always to be a concord.

EXAMPLE

To which may be referred all kinds of breakings or dividings, either of the bass itself or of the descant that is joined to it, of which you may

---

[1] Chapters 2–5 are similar in content and treatment to material to be found in Simpson's book, *The Division-Viol*, Part II. (See Introduction, pp. xxxv and xxxvi, and footnote 3 on p. 19 and footnote 14 on p. 24.)

[2] The first note of the bar, not the seventh degree of the scale.

see hundreds of examples in my book named *The Division-Viol*, 3rd Part, the whole discourse being upon that subject.[3]

Here again take notice that two, three or more notes standing together in the same line or space may be considered as one entire note and may admit a discord to be joined to any of them, the first only excepted.

EXAMPLE

Although in this example I show what liberty you have to use discords where many notes stand together in the same line or space, which may properly be used in vocal music where both the parts pronounce the same words or syllables together, yet it is not very usual in music made for instruments.

3. OF SYNCOPATION

The other way in which discords are not only allowed or admitted, but of most excellent use and ornament in composition, is in syncopation or binding. That is, when a note of one part ends and breaks off upon the middle of the note of another part, as you see in the following examples.

[3] A good example of breaking a ground is to be found on p. 33 of *The Division-Viol*. Part of this example is given below:

Syncopation in Two Parts

These examples do show you all the bindings or syncopations that are usually to be found, as 7ths with 6ths, 6ths with 5ths, 4ths with 3rd, 3rds with 2nds. Why 8ves and 5ths are exempt from binding with their neighbouring discords shall presently appear.[4]

In this way of binding, a discord may be applied to the first part of any note of the bass if the other part of the binding note did sound

---

[4] See the second paragraph of Chapter 4, 'Passage of Discords.'

Syncopation in Three Parts

in concordance to that note of the bass which went before, and some-times also without that qualification wherein some skill or judgement is required.

4. PASSAGE OF DISCORDS

Discords thus admitted, we are next to consider how they are brought off to render them delightful, for simply of themselves they are harsh and displeasing to the ear and introduced into music only for variety, or by striking the sense with a disproportionate sound to beget a greater attention to that which follows, to the hearing whereof we are drawn on, as it were, by a vehement expectation.

This winding or bringing a discord off is always best effected by changing from thence into some imperfect concord, to which more sweetness seems to be added by the discord sounding before it. And

[5] The above examples would no doubt fall under the heading of suspensions in a modern textbook. The disturbing of the normal flow of the beat for short periods in individual part is technically syncopation resulting in suspended discords. Coperario discusses suspensions and syncopated notes together in *Rules How to Compose*, under the unfortunate heading 'Of Ligatures.'

here you have the reason why an 8ve and a 5th do not admit of syncopation or binding with their neighbouring discords because a 7th doth pass more pleasingly into a 6th, as also a 9th into a 10th or 3rd. And as for a 5th, though it bind well enough with a 6th, as you did see in some of the foregoing examples, yet with a 4th it will not bind so well because a 4th doth pass more properly into a 3rd.

These little windings and bindings with discords and imperfect concords after them do very much delight the ear, yet do not satisfy it but hold it in suspense, as it were, until they come to a perfect concord, where, as at a period, we understand the sense of that which went before.

Now in passing from discords to imperfect concords, we commonly remove to that which is nearest, rather than to one that is more remote, which rule holds good also in passing from imperfect concords to those that are more perfect.

5. OF DISCORDS, NOTE AGAINST NOTE

Although we have mentioned but two ways in which discords are allowed, that is in diminution and syncopation, yet we find a third way wherein skilful composers do often use them, which is by setting note for note of the same quantity one against another. And though it be against the common rules of composition, yet being done with judgement and design, it may be ranked amongst the elegances of figurate music.

The prime or chief of which, for their use and excellency in music, are a tritone and a semidiapente, that is the greater or excessive 4th and the lesser or defective 5th. Which according to the scale, where we have no other divisions or distinctions than semitones or half-notes, seem to be the same interval as to proportion of sound, either of them consisting of six semitones; but their appearance in practice is one of them as a 4th, the other like a 5th, which if placed one above the other, complete the compass of an octave in manner following:

Their use in figurate descant is very frequent both in syncopation and note against note as in counterpoint. The tritone passes naturally into a 6th, the semidiapente into a 3rd, thus:

The parts or sounds which they usually require to be joined with them, either in binding or without it, are a second above the lower note of the tritone and a second above the higher note of the semi-diapente, which makes that 6th we mentioned, page 30, as necessary to be joined with an imperfect 5th.

EXAMPLE

(6)

6. Of Discords in double Transition

I showed you formerly (page 33) how a note is sometimes broken to make a transition by degrees to some other concord.

These transitions or breakings are commonly expressed in quavers or crotchets, sometimes (though seldom) in minims. The examples I gave you were set for the treble but may be applied to the bass also or any other part.

Now if the bass and an upper part do both make a transition at the same time in notes of the same quantity and in contrary motion which is their usual passage, there must of necessity be an encounter of discords whilst either part proceeds by degrees toward its designed concord. And therefore in such a passage, discords no doubt may be allowed note against note.

[6] The examples referring to the tritone and semidiapente (excepting those illustrating the semitones contained within the intervals) are on single staves and engraved in the early editions. All other musical examples in the book are printed from movable type. Type printing was most suitable for musical examples which had a single part to each stave, but not for chords. To avoid printing costs these examples were engraved. They are taken from *The Division-Viol*, p. 22 (see Introduction, p. xxxv), but the same examples in this book are made up from specially made type. The reason for not using the type of *The Division-Viol* examples for the *Compendium* examples was probably that both books were being printed at the same time. Both the second edition of *The Division-Viol* and the second edition of the *Compendium* date from 1667. (See Introduction, p. xx.)

EXAMPLE

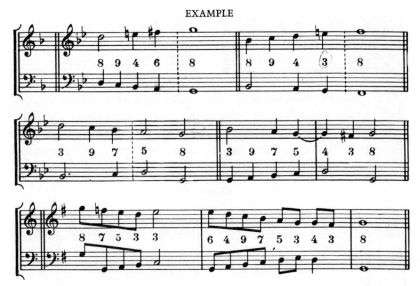

Besides these which depend upon the rule of breaking and transition, there may be other ways wherein a skilful composer may upon design set a discord, for which no general rule is to be given, and therefore not to be exhibited to a beginner, there being a great difference betwixt that which is done with judgement and design and that which is committed by oversight or ignorance. Again, many things may be allowed in quavers and crotchets, as in these examples that I have shown, which would not be so allowable in minims or semibreves.

I told you formerly that discords are best brought off when they pass into imperfect concords[7] which is true doctrine and ought to be observed (as much as may be) in long notes and syncopation. But in short notes and diminution we are not so strictly obliged to observance of that rule. Neither can we ascend or descend by degrees to a 5th or to an 8ve but a 4th will come before the one and a 7th before the other.

Again, a 7th doth properly pass into a 5th when the parts do meet in contrary motion, as you may see in the example next following:

[7] The second paragraph of Chapter 4, 'Passage of Discords,' in Part III.

And here you may see two 7ths, both parts descending, betwixt the bass and higher treble, not by oversight but set with design.

7. OF RELATION INHARMONICAL

After this discourse of discords I think it very proper to say something concerning relation inharmonical which I formerly did but only mention.

Relation or respect or reference inharmonical is a harsh reflection of flat against sharp in a cross form, that is, when the present note of one part, compared with the foregoing note of another part, doth produce some harsh and displeasing discord. Examples of it are such as follow:

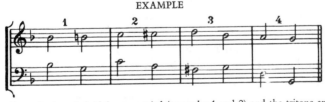

The first note of the treble is E natural[9] which, considered crosswise with the second note of the bass in E flat, begets the sound of a lesser second which is a discord. The second example is the same descending.

The third example, comparing E natural in the bass with B flat in the treble, produces a false 5th which is also a discord. The like may be said of the fourth example.

The first note of the bass in the fifth example stands in B flat which, compared with the last note of the treble in E natural, produces the sound of a tritone or greater 4th which is also a harsh discord.

Though these cross relations sound not both together, yet they leave a harshness in the ear which is to be avoided, especially in composition of few parts.

But you must know that this cross reflection of flat against sharp doth not always produce relation inharmonical.

EXAMPLE

[8] The major and minor 3rd of the same triad (examples 1 and 2) and the tritone and semi-diapente (examples 3–5) are the worst of the false relations. Yet false relations frequently occur in the works of sixteenth-century composers, although as the century progressed, the use of them became less frequent in the works of continental composers. English musicians, however, employed strong cross relations with little concern.

[9] See footnote 25 on p. 29.

For it is both usual and proper for the upper part to change from flat to sharp when the bass doth fall a lesser 3rd, as you see in the first and second bars of this example. Also, that reflection of F sharp against B flat in the third bar, which produces the sound of a lesser 4th, is not relation inharmonical.[10] The reason thereof you shall presently have. But first I will give you a clearer instance thereof by comparing it with another 4th, flat against sharp crosswise, that your own ear may better judge what is and what is not relation inharmonical.

EXAMPLE

The first two instances show a relation of F sharp in the bass against B flat in the treble which begets the sound of a lesser 4th and is very good and usual in composition. The other two instances are F natural in the bass against B natural in the treble which makes a greater or excessive 4th, a very harsh relation. And here, by the way, you may observe three different 4ths in practical music, viz. (1) from F sharp to B flat upward, (2) from F natural to B flat, and (3) from F natural to B natural, thus exemplified:

As to the reason why F sharp against B flat doth not produce relation inharmonical, we are to consider the proportion of its interval, which indeed belongs rather to the theory of music, for though the ear informs a practical composer which sounds are harsh or pleasing, it is the speculative part that considers the reason why such or such intervals make those sounds which please or displease the ear.

But we will reduce this business of the lesser 4th into practice, that thereby we may give a reason to a practical musician why it falls not under relation inharmonical. To which purpose, we will examine it according to our common scale of music and there we shall find it to consist of no more than four semitones or half notes, which is the very same number that makes a ditone or greater 3rd. Example will render it more plain.

[10] Zarlino regards the diminished 4th favourably. He treats the subject of false relation at some length in Book Three of *Institutioni Armoniche* (1558) forbidding false relations in two parts but permitting the cross relation of the diminished 4th. The relevant passage is given in translation in Strunk, *op. cit.*, p. 243. 'But when the relationship is that of the semidiatessaron, and it occurs between accidental signs, such as the ♯ and the ♭, or when only one of these signs is present, we need not avoid it at all, for the two divisions being harmonic it is obvious that they will make a good effect, even though they are not varied.'

Now I suppose that no practical musician will say that the two
terms of a greater 3rd have any harsh relation one to the other, which
granted, doth also exempt the other (being the like interval) from
relation inharmonical, though in appearance it be a 4th and hath flat
against sharp in cross reflection.

By this you may perceive that distances in the scale are not always
the same in sound which they seem to the sight. To illustrate this a
little further we will add a lesser 3rd to the former lesser 4th, which
in appearance will make a lesser 6th, for so the degrees in the scale will
exhibit it in manner following:

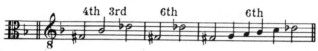

But this 6th in sight is no more in sound than a common 5th, which
we may demonstrate by the scale itself. For if we remove each term
a semitone lower, which must needs keep them still at the same distance, we shall find the 6th changed into a 5th in sight as well as sound,
and the lesser 4th likewise changed into a greater 3rd, as you may see
in this example:

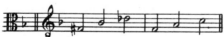

And if we remove the latter three notes again and set them a semitone higher by adding a sharp to each note, thus,

that which in the first instance was D flat is now become C sharp, and
·likewise B flat now changed into A sharp.

This removing of the concords a semitone higher or lower, as also
the changing them into keys which have no affinity with the cardinal
key upon which the air of the music dependeth, does many times cause
an untunableness in the concords as though our strings were out of
tune when we play upon instruments which have fixed stops or frets.
And this also happens amongst the keys of harpsichords and organs,
the reason whereof is the inequality of tones and semitones, either of
them having their major and minor which our common scale doth not

distinguish.[11] And this has caused some to complain against the scale itself as though it were defective. Concerning which I will presume no further than the delivering of my own opinion, to which purpose I must first say something—

8. OF THE THREE SCALES OF MUSIC

The three scales are these: 1. Scala Diatonica, 2. Scala Cromatica, 3. Scala Enharmonica. The diatonic scale is that which rises to a 5th by three tones and a semitone and from thence to the 8ve by two tones and one semitone, which semitone is denoted in both places by Fa as I showed in the beginning of this treatise.

EXAMPLE

This is in effect the old Grecian scale consisting of four tetrachords or 4ths extending to a double octave which Guido Aretinus, a monk of St. Benedict's Order (about the year of our Lord 960) changed into a form in which it now is, setting this Greek letter Γ Gamma at the bottom of it to acknowledge from whence he had it,[12] and this, for its general use, is now called the common scale of music.

The chromatic scale rises to a 5th by a tone and five semitones and from thence proceeds to an 8ve by five semitones more.[13]

EXAMPLE

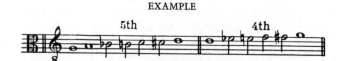

Some perhaps may find fault with this example of the chromatic scale as being not the usual way of setting it down, but I thought it

[11] Until about 1740, when equal temperament was applied to the scale, various tunings were employed at different ages. Mean tone temperament was first used about 1500. Schlick, in *Spiegel der Orgelmacher und Organisten*, 1511, based a system of tuning on a 5th which was slightly smaller (approximately 1/34 tone) than the perfect 5th. The 5ths when tuned in this way, F-c, c-g, g-d', d'-a', resulted in a' making a perfect 3rd with two octaves above F. Although combining the notes of this scale into triads gave excellent results in keys of not more than one or two sharps or flats, there were unfortunate consequences when the succession of 5ths was extended, and discrepancies occurred between the pitch of notes which were enharmonically equivalent, e.g. G#, A♭, C#, D♭, D#. E♭. This system was also discussed by Zarlino and by Francis Salinas, the blind Professor of Music in the University of Salamanca, in his *De Musica libri septem*, 1577.   [12] See footnote 2 on p. 1.
[13] The note g# a♭ is not included in this scale but Simpson himself uses g#s and a♭s in the examples and in the appendix. This note is also omitted in the musical example on p. 56.

the best instance I could give a learner of it as to its use in practical music in which it is so frequently mixed with the diatonic scale that the ♭ flat and ♯ sharp which formerly belonged to B only have now got the names of the chromatic signs by their frequent application to notes in all places of the scale, and music which moves much in semitones or half notes is commonly called chromatic music. And from hence it is that an octave is divided into 12 semitones.

The enharmonic scale rises gradually by dieses or quarter notes, of which 24 make up an octave and is so far out of use that we scarce know how to give an example of it. Those who endeavour it do set it down in this manner.[14]

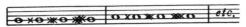

But as to its use in practical music I am yet to seek, for I do not conceive how a natural voice can ascend or descend by such minute degrees and hit them right in tune. Neither do I see how syncopes or bindings with discords, which are the chief ornaments of composition, can be performed by quarter-notes. Or how the concords, by them, can be removed from key to key without much trouble and confusion. For these reasons I am slow to believe that any good music, especially of many parts, can be composed by quarter-notes, although I hear some talk much of it.

Only one place there is where I conceive a quarter-note might serve instead of a semitone which is in the binding cadence of the Greater 3rd, and that, commonly, is covered or drowned either by the trill of the voice or shake of the finger.

But some do fancy that as the diatonic scale is made more elegant by a mixture of the chromatic, so likewise it might be bettered by help of the enharmonic scale in such places where those little dissonances do occur.

I do not deny but that the slitting of the keys in harpsichords and organs, as also the placing of a middle fret near the top or nut of a viol or theorbo where the space is wide, may be useful in some cases for the sweetening of such dissonances as may happen in those places; but I do not conceive that the enharmonic scale is therein concerned, seeing

---

[14] A hundred years earlier, Vicentino had attempted a revival of quarter tone music. In *L'antica musica*, 1555, and *Descrizione dell' arciorgano*, 1561, he gives an account of a harpsichord which had 31 keys to the octave, employing quarter tones. It could produce all the tones of the three Greek scales, diatonic, chromatic and enharmonic. But the quarter tones occurred only between certain notes in the scale, not between all the semitones as Simpson's example would lead us to believe.

those dissonances are sometimes more, sometimes less, and seldom that any of them do hit precisely the quarter of a note.[15]

Now as to my opinion concerning our common scale of music, taking it with its mixture of the chromatic, I think it lies not in the wit of man to frame a better as to all intents and purposes for practical music. And as for those little dissonances (for so I call them for want of a better word to express them) the fault is not in the scale, whose office and design is no more than to denote the distances of the concords and discords according to the lines and spaces of which it doth consist, and to show by what degrees of tones and semitones a voice may rise or fall.

For in vocal music those dissonances are not perceived, neither do they occur in instruments which have no frets as violins and wind instruments where the sound is modulated by the touch of the finger; but in such only as have fixed stops or frets, which being placed and fitted for the most usual keys in the scale, seem out of order when we change to keys less usual, and that (as I said) doth happen by reason of the inequality of tones and semitones, especially of the latter.

Concerning which, I shall (with submission to better judgements) adventure to deliver my own sense and opinion. And though it belongs more properly to the mathematical part of music, yet happily a practical explanation thereof may give some satisfaction to a practical musician when he shall see and understand the reason.

9. OF GREATER AND LESSER SEMITONES[16]

First you must know that sounds have their proportions as well as numbers.

Those proportions may be explained by a line divided in 2, 3, 4, 5, or more equal parts. We will suppose that line to be the string of a lute or viol. Take which string you please so it be true, but the smallest is fittest for the purpose.

---

[15] Praetorius mentions in his *Syntagma musicum*, 1624, a keyboard instrument called the Universal–clavicymbal, built by Charles Luythorn, 1556–1620, a Belgian, which had eighteen notes to the octave. They were c, c♯, d♭, d, d♯, e♭, e, e♯, f, f♯, g♭, g, g♯, a♭, a, b♭, b, b♯ (See footnote 14 on p. 51.) This facilitated modulation without resorting to the system of equal temperament. Many sixteenth–century organs had these divided keys. This method removed the discordant elements which accompanied such modulations, but, as Simpson points out, had little to do with the enharmonic. The c♯ between the c and d♭ was not a quarter tone removed·from these two notes. For a detailed examination of the mean tone system, see Alexander Wood, *The Physics of Music*, London, 1944, pp. 190–192.

[16] In the true scale based on the perfect 5th, there resulted two different kinds of tone, the major and the minor, and two different kinds of semitone. The mean tone system, based on a smaller 5th, came to be accepted in the seventeenth century and replaced the two different tones by adding half their difference to the minor tone, resulting in a tone whose pitch lay midway between that of the minor tone and the major tone. Two different sizes of semitone were still distinguished, however. As Simpson mentions the greater and lesser tone (p. 53) it is obvious that he is discussing temperament prior to the mean tone system. The mean tone system was not universally adopted until the end of the seventeenth century.

Divide the length of that string from the nut to the bridge into two equal parts, stop it in the middle and you will hear the sound of an octave if you compare it with the sound of the open string. Therefore is a diapason said to be in dupla proportion to its octave.

Next divide the string into three equal parts and stop that part next the nut which will be at the fret h if rightly placed, compare the sound thereof with the open string and you will hear the difference to be a 5th. Thence is a 5th said to be Sesquialtera proportion, that is, as 2 is to 3.

Again, divide the string into four equal parts, stop that part next the nut (which will be at the f fret) and you have a 4th to the open string. Therefore a 4th is said to be Sesquitertia Proportion, as 3 is to 4. By these you may conceive the rest towards the nut.

If you ask me concerning the other half of the string from the middle to the bridge, the middle of that half makes another octave, and so every middle one after another.

We will now come a little nearer to our business of the semitones. To which purpose we must divide the octave itself into equal parts. First, in the middle, which will fall upon the fret f. Examine the sound from f to n (which is octave to the open string) and you will find it to be a 5th. Try the other half which is towards the nut and you will hear it is but a 4th.

Next, divide that 5th which is from f to n into two equal parts and you will find that half which is towards the bridge to be a greater 3rd and the other half to the nut-ward to be a lesser 3rd.

Then divide that greater 3rd into two equal parts and you will have a greater and a lesser tone. Lastly, divide that greater tone (which was that half next the bridge) into two equal parts and you have a greater and a lesser semitone, the greater being always that half which is nearer to the bridge.

By this you may perceive that all our musical intervals arise from the division of a line or string into equal parts, and that those equal parts do still produce unequal sounds. And this is the very reason that we have greater and lesser semitones.[17]

[17] It was Pythagoras who discovered that the division of a stretched string into segments whose relationship with each other could be expressed by a simple numerical ratio, produced notes which were related to a fundamental. Simpson included this information in his book, knowing that he would be likely to be criticized for his pains (see his preface, paragraph 5). It was the kind of knowledge in which the mediaeval theorist and the erudite scholar of the seventeenth century delighted. In the seventeenth century the mean tone system of tuning was replacing the older method. Why Simpson did not attempt to acquaint himself with the more recent methods of temperament, since he was running a certain risk in treating the subject anyway, is surprising. It is even more surprising that the passage remained unaltered in subsequent editions. The ninth edition, published about 1790, contains the same passage, by this time completely out of date due to the replacing of the mean tone system by equal temperament.

Thereupon is a tone or whole note, as we term it, divided into nine particles called Commas, five of which are assigned to the greater semitone and four to the less. The difference betwixt them is called Apotome, which signifies a cutting off. Some authors call the greater semitone, Apotome, that is, I suppose, because it includes the odd Comma which makes that Apotome. Thus you see a tone or note divided into a greater and lesser half, but how to divide it into two equal halves I never see determined.

The famous Kircher in his learned and elaborate *Musurgia Universalis*, page 103,[18] treating of the mathematical part of music, which he handles more clearly and largely than any author I think that ever wrote upon that subject, doth show us the type of a tone cut in the middle by dividing the middle Comma into two schisms. But that Comma, being divided arithmetically, will have its greater and a lesser half (as to sound) as well as any greater interval so divided.

The nearest instance I can give you of a sound parted in the middle is an octave divided into a Tritone and a Semidiapente, either of them consisting of six semitones as I showed, page 44, and yet there is some little difference in their ratios or habitudes.

I will give you yet a clearer instance by which you may see what different sounds will arise from one division of a line or string into equal parts. To which purpose, divide that 5th which is from the nut to h fret into two equal parts with a pair of compasses (the middle whereof will hit upon d fret, if it be not placed with some abatement for the reasons forementioned) and you will find that the same wideness of the compass which divided the 5th in the middle and so made a greater and a lesser 3rd, the same wideness, I say, applied from h towards the bridge, will, in the first place from h, produce a 4th, in the next place, a 5th, and in the next after that, an 8ve, according to this line:

Nut	Less 3rd	Great 3rd	Fourth	Fifth	Octave		Bridge
a		d	h	n	v		

But seeing you cannot conveniently hear the sound of that 8ve, it being so near the bridge, take the wideness of the 5th from the nut to h and you will find that the same wideness which makes a 5th doth make an 8ve in the next place after it according to this line:

Nut	Fifth	Octave		Bridge
a		h	v	

---

[18] Athanasius Kircher, 1602–1680, *Musurgia universalis sive ars magna consoni et dissone*, 2 vols., Rome, 1650. This work contains much information on the nature of sound and principles of composition. It is frequently inaccurate. Simpson refers to this book again in the *Compendium* on p. 68.

If you please to try these distances upon the treble string of a Bass-Viol, you will have a production of these sounds:

By this you may perceive that every equal division of a line or string doth still produce a greater interval of sound as it approaches nearer to the bridge. And by this which hath been shown, I suppose you see not only the reason but necessity of greater and lesser semitones. Our next business is to examine—

10. WHERE THESE GREATER AND LESSER SEMITONES ARISE IN THE SCALE OF MUSIC

This depends upon the key in which a song is set, and upon the division of its 5th into the greater and lesser 3rd, and the placing of these which determines whether the key be flat or sharp[19] as hath been shown. We will suppose the key to be in G.

The diatonic scale hath only two places in each octave in which a semitone takes place. One is in rising to the 5th, the other in rising from thence to the 8ve, and these two places are known by the note Fa as formerly shown. These two sounds denoted by Fa are always the lesser semitone from that degree which is next under them. So that from A to B flat is a lesser semitone and betwixt B flat and B natural, which makes the difference of the lesser and greater 3rd, is (or ought to be) always the greater semitone. The like may be understood of the higher Fa.

I know that some authors do place the greater semitone from A to B flat and the lesser betwixt B flat and B natural, but I adhere to the other opinion as the more rational to my understanding.[20]

By this you see where greater and lesser semitones take place in the

---

[19] = major or minor.

[20] Simpson here shows his preference for the older method of tuning. The 'authors' he mentions are those who are advocating mean tone temperament. If the octave (c-c') contains 300 savarts, the 6th (a) and the seventh (b♮), measured according to the Pythagorean scale contain 226.5 and 277.5 savarts respectively. The minor 7th (b♭), a full tone below c', contains 300s — 51s = 249s. Therefore the interval a — b♭ contains 249s — 226.5s = 22.5s (lesser semitone) and the interval b♭ — b♮ contains 277.5s — 249s = 28.5s (greater semitone). This explains Simpson's placing of the greater and lesser semitones.

The 'authors,' measuring their intervals according to mean tone temperament, have a 6th (a) and a seventh (b♮) containing 222.4s and 270.7s respectively. The interval a — b♭ contains 251.7s — 222.4s = 29.3s (greater semitone) and the interval b♭ — b♮ contains 270.7s — 251.7s = 19s (lesser semitone). Thus:

Simpson (Pythagorean scale) a — b♭ = 22.5s (lesser semitone)
b♭ — b♮ = 28.5s (greater semitone)
'Authors' (Mean tone scale) a — b♭ = 29.3s (greater semitone)
b♭ — b♮ = 19s (lesser semitone)

diatonic scale. We will now cast our eye upon them as they rise in
the chromatic, according to the example I gave you of it. In which
the greater and lesser half-notes do follow each other successively, as
shall be here denoted by two letters, l for lesser and g for greater.

EXAMPLE

Now if we should remove this example a semitone higher or lower,
the lesser semitones would fall in the places of the greater, and contrarily, the greater in the places of the lesser, which transposition is the
chief cause of those little disonances which occasioned this discourse.[21]

Your best way to avoid them is to set your music in the usual and
most natural keys of the scale.

[21] Instrumental music from about 1600 to 1820 was pitched lower than that of the present:
the a' of those days was slightly below our present g♯. See R. T. Dart, *The Interpretation of
Music*, London, 1954, p. 55.

THE FOURTH PART

TEACHING THE FORM OF FIGURATE DESCANT

1. What is meant by Figurate Descant[1]

FIGURATE DESCANT is that wherein discords are concerned as well as concords. And as we termed Plain Descant (in which was taught the use of the concords) the groundwork or grammar of musical composition, so may we properly nominate this the ornament or rhetorical part of music. For in this are introduced all the varieties of points, fugues,[2] syncopes or bindings, diversities of measures, intermixtures of discording sounds, or what else art and fancy can exhibit, which as different flowers and figures do set forth and adorn the composition, whence it is named Melothesia florida vel figurata, Florid or Figurate Descant.

2. Of the Greek Modes[3] and Latin Tones

Before we treat of Figurate Descant, I must not omit to say something concerning the Modes or Tones. Not so much for any great use we have of them as to let you know what is meant by them and that I may not appear singular, for you shall scarce meet with any author that has writ[ten] of music but you will read something concerning them.

The Modes we mentioned in the first part of this treatise were in reference to notes and measure of time. These are concerning Tune.

That which the Grecians called Mode or Mood the Latins termed Tone or Tune. The design of either was to show in what key a song was set and which keys had affinity one with another. The Greeks distinguished their Modes by the names of their provinces, as Doric, Lydian, Ionic, Phrygian, etc. The Latins reduced theirs to eight

---

[1] The word figurate or figured was used in the seventeenth and eighteenth centuries to describe music which contained short figures or motives, but the term was unfortunately loosely applied. Figured bass is another use of the same word. The word descant was used during the same period in musical treatises to mean instruction in counterpoint. Discant was used in the same sense in the thirteenth and fourteenth centuries, originally meaning that musical style which was in several parts and in modal rhythm as opposed to the free rhythm of the organal style. The title of the fourth part of the *Compendium* might therefore be more clearly described as The Teaching of Florid Counterpoint.

[2] Simpson writes *fuges*. This has been changed to fugues, here and elsewhere.

[3] Simpson refers to the *Greek Moods*, and spells the names of them, *Dorick, Lidian, Ionick, Phrigian*.

plainsong tunes and those were set in the tenor, so called because it was the holding part to which they did apply their descant.[4]

These plainsongs did seldom exceed the compass of six notes or degrees of sound and therefore were Ut and Re (as I suppose) applied to the two lowest that each degree might have a several appellation; otherwise, four names, as now we use, viz. Mi, Fa, Sol, La, had been both more easy and more suitable to the ancient scale which consisted of tetrachords or 4ths, two of which made up the compass of an octave.

From these six notes, Ut, Re, Mi, Fa, Sol, La, did arise three properties of singing which they named B Quarre, B Molle, and Properchant or Natural. B Quarre was when they sang Mi in B, that clef being then made of a square form, thus, ♮ , and set at the beginning of the lines as we now set some one of the other three clefs. B Molle was when they sung Fa in B. Properchant was when their Ut was applied to C so that their six notes did not reach so high as to touch B, either flat or natural. But in our modern music we acknowledge no such thing as Properchant, every song being of its own nature either flat or sharp,[5] and that determined not by B's flat or natural, but by the greater or lesser 3rd being joined next to the key in which any song is set.[6]

These Modes or Tones had yet another distinction and that was Authentic or Plagal. This depended upon the dividing of the octave into its 5th and 4th. Authentic was when the 5th stood in the lower place according to the harmonical division of an octave. Plagal was when the 5th possessed the upper place according to the arithmetical division thereof.

Authentic   EXAMPLE   Plagal

Harmonical   Arihmetical

Many volumes have been written about these Modes or Tones concerning their use, their number, nature, and affinity one with another; and yet the business left imperfect or obscure as to any certain

---

[4] Simpson's account of the modes is sketchy and misleading. His description is confined to the twelve church modes as first mentioned by Glareanus in his *Dodekachordon*, 1552, and Simpson has confused this mediaeval system with that of the Greeks. Although certain similarities occur between the two systems, the distinguishing features make it clear that he knew little of the Greek system and his account shows an inadequate knowledge of the church modes.

[5] = minor or major key.

[6] This very brief discussion of the hexachord system is equally misleading since it comes under the heading of modes. As Simpson was aware of the importance of Guido d'Arezzo in the history of musical theory (see p. 1 and p. 50) it is unfortunate that he should place Guido's very important contribution to mediaeval theory under the general heading of Greek modes.

rule for regulating the key and air of the music though one of the greatest concerns of musical composition.

Mr. Morley upon this subject in his *Introduction to Music*, page 147, his scholar making this query, 'Have you no general rule to be given for an instruction for keeping of the key?' answers, 'No, for it must proceed only of the judgement of the composer, yet (saith he) the churchmen for keeping of their keys have devised certain notes commonly called the Eight Tunes,' etc., of which he only gives examples and so leaves the business.[7] And no marvel they could give no certain rule so long as they took their sight from the tenor, in which case it must of necessity be left to the judgement of the composer or singer of descant what bass he will apply unto it. But according to the method formerly delivered in this treatise where we make the bass the foundation of the harmony, upon which the key solely depends as also the other keys which have affinity therewith, the business is reduced to a certainty of rule, both plain and easy (see page 22, Concerning the Key or Tone). And though in Figurate Descant we often have occasion to apply undernotes to an upper part, as you will see hereafter, yet the whole conduct of the composition, as to the key and middle closes thereto belonging, is the very same and therefore to be observed according to what we there delivered.

I give you this brief account of the Modes and Tones that you might not be wholly ignorant of anything that belongs to music; to which purpose I have contrived this little table, collected out of such authors as number 12 Tones or Tunes answerable to the Grecian Modes, to wit, six Authentic and six Plagal.

Authentic		*Plagal*	
D	1. Doric	2.	Hypo-Doric
E	3. Phrygian	4.	Hypo-Phrygian
F	5. Lydian	6.	Hypo-Lydian
G	7. Mixolydian	8.	Hypo-Mixolydian
A	9. Aeolian	10.	Hypo-Aeolian
C	11. Ionic	12.	Hypo-Ionic

The first column shows the keys in the scale of music to which those Tones and Modes are assigned. The second expresses the order of the Authentic Tones, known by their odd numbers, as 1, 3, 5, etc. The third column contains the names of the Grecian Authentic Modes. The

---

[7] Morley, *op. cit.* (ed. by R. A. Harman), p. 249. But Morley is careful to point out in the same paragraph, 'And these [the 'Eight Tunes'] be, although not the true substance, yet some shadow of the ancient "modi" whereof Boethius and Glareanus have written so much.' Simpson has also failed to notice that although Morley 'so leaves the business' at that point in the text, the Annotations upon the Third Part of Morley's book (pp. 300–304) are devoted to the discussion of the modes. The word *Tunes* is probably derived from Tones which seems to have been the accepted word for the modes in the sixteenth century.

fourth shows the Plagal Tones, known always by their even numbers, as 2, 4, 6, etc. The last or fifth column contains the names of the Grecian Plagal Modes, distinguished by the particle Hypo.

Where you may observe that B mi is exempt from having any Tone or Mode assigned to it, because F fa doth make an Imperfect 5th thereto. Howbeit, B fa is become a key or Tone now much in use, especially in music composed for instruments.

But whereas we read such strange and marvellous things of the various affections and different effects of the Grecian Modes, we may very probably conjecture that it proceeded chiefly from their having Modes of different measure joined with them, which we find by experience doth make that vast difference betwixt light and grave music, though both set in the same key and consequently the same Mode or Tone.[8]

3. OF FIGURATE MUSIC IN GENERAL

Figurate Descant, as I told you, is that wherein discords are concerned as well, though not so much, as concords. You have already been taught the use of both in composition, and these are the two materials which must serve you for the raising of all structures in Figurate Music.

To give you models at large of all those several structures were to write a great volume, not a Compendium. It will be sufficient that I let you see the form of Figurate Descant and that I give you some short examples of such things as are of most concern with instructions, so near as I can, for their contrivance. We will begin with setting a bass to a treble, as we formerly did with making a treble to a bass.

4. HOW TO SET A BASS TO A TREBLE

In this you must reckon your concords from the treble downward as in the other you did from the bass upward, which is but the same thing in effect; for a 3rd, 5th, 6th and 8ve, are still the same whether you reckon them·upward or downward.

But whereas in plain counterpoint I did order the bass to move on for the most part by leaps of a 3rd, 4th, 5th, etc., which indeed is the most proper movement of the bass in that kind of composition, here you must know that in Figurate Descant those leaps are frequently changed or broken into degrees, as you may easily conceive by this example.

---

[8] The ethos of the Greek modes, that is, the association of mood and character with each mode, e.g. strength with the Dorian, sadness with the Mixolydian, was also evident in the church modes according to seventeenth-century theorists. Diruta in *Il Transilvano*, II, 1609, gives details of these associations. Again it is presumably the church modes and not the Grecian modes to which Simpson refers.

And therefore it is left to your liberty to use either the one or the other as occasion shall require. Only take notice that if in these breakings the parts do ascend or descend together by degrees, it must be either in 3rds or 6ths. If they move contrary by degrees, that is one rising, the other falling, you have liberty to pass through discords as well as concords according to what I showed of discords, note against note.⁹ For the rest, I refer you to the principles formerly delivered in composition of two parts. And if your treble do chance to hold out any long note, you may let the bass during the time pass on from one imperfect concord to another, as from a 3rd to a 6th, or the contrary. The like may be understood of the treble when the bass holds out a note.

EXAMPLE

Also your composition will be more neat if you can use some formality in your bass by imitating and answering the notes of the treble in such places as will admit it.

We will now suppose a treble made by some other person, as indeed this was which I am about to write down (made by a person of quality)¹² and given to have a bass set to it.

Here you see the bass still answering and imitating the treble, so near as the rules of composition do permit, sometimes in the octave, as you see in most part of the first strain, and sometimes in other distances, as you may observe in the beginning of the second strain, but still keeping close to the rules of composition which must be chiefly observed. This is as much as I think necessary for setting a bass to a treble.

⁹ See p. 45.

¹⁰ From the bass line it would appear that Simpson is discussing instrumental counterpoint although he makes no mention of the fact save that there is no naming of the parts as in the previous vocal examples. The longer musical examples in this fourth part of the book, are presumably written for stringed instruments. Simpson is keeping abreast of his times in teaching both vocal and instrumental composition.

¹¹ The C in the lower part at the end of the first bar, making a discord with the upper part, is quitted by the leap of an augmented 5th. The same progression may be seen in the example on p. 62, where the middle part moves from c' to f♯ in the third bar.

¹² Probably Mathew Locke. Simpson acknowledges his obligations to Locke on p. 90.

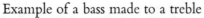

Example of a bass made to a treble

And by this you may perceive how different the form and movement of the parts in Figurate Descant is from that of plain counterpoint. For in that, the natural passage of the treble is for the most part by degrees; in this, you may use what leaps you please so they be airy and formal.

5. How Parts pass through one another

Again, in counterpoint, each part does ordinarily move within its own sphere. In Figurate Descant, the parts do frequently mix and pass through one another, insomuch that if there be two trebles, you shall have sometimes this, sometimes that, above or below, as you see in the following instances:

[13] The pauses at the end of this example do not indicate that the notes are to be held on for more than their written values. See footnote 21 on p. 13.

The like may be understood of the inner parts or of the basses when the composition is designed for two. Howbeit, the highest part for the time being is still to be accounted the treble, and the lowest part, whatever it be, is (during that time) the bass to all the parts that stand above it.

Lastly, whereas in counterpoint I commended unto you the joining of your upper parts so close together that no other part could be put in amongst them, in Figurate Music (especially for instruments) that rule is not so strictly observed, but each part doth commonly move according to the compass of the voice or instrument for which it is intended. But the principles of composition, as the choosing, ordering and placing of the concords, are the very same we delivered in plain counterpoint; that is to say, in two or three parts you are to avoid 8ves, except in such places as there mentioned. In four or more parts, you are to dispose those parts into several concords as much as you can with convenience.

6. CONCERNING THE CONSECUTION OF PERFECTS OF THE SAME KIND, AND OF OTHER DISALLOWANCES IN COMPOSITION[14]

I told you (page 21) that perfects of the same kind, as two 5ths or two 8ves rising or falling together, were not allowed in composition.

[14] See the Editor's Preface. In the second edition, chapter 6 is Concerning the Consecution of 4th and 5ths,' i.e. chapter 7 in the third edition. Therefore Part IV of the second edition of the book contains 14 chapters and Part IV of the third edition contains 15 chapters.

This is not the only discrepancy at this place and the third edition version is given in the text of the present edition. Following the 6th chapter-heading in the second edition is a paragraph which is not to be found in the third edition. It is quoted below:

'6. CONCERNING THE CONSECUTION OF 4TH AND 5THS

Three parts cannot ascend or descend by degrees together but there will be a consecution of so many 4ths betwixt some two of the upper parts. And if we transpose those two parts by placing the lower an octave higher or setting the higher an octave lower, those 4ths will be changed into 5ths as you see in these following instances.'

This paragraph is very like the two paragraphs which precede the musical example on p. 67.

The above quotation is followed in the second edition by the musical example on p. 67 showing the three 4ths between the alto and tenor and the three 5ths between treble and tenor. In the second edition, the first part of this example reads:

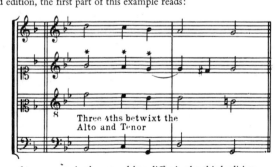

The soprano and tenor parts in the second bar differ in the third edition.

The text is resumed after this musical example with the paragraph beginning, 'The question now is whether these three 5ths. . . .' The paragraph immediately following this musical example in the third edition beginning, 'The notes transposed are those of the tenor . . .' is not to be found in the second edition.

Also (page 22) I showed some other passages prohibited in few, that is to say, in two or three parts. Here I will give you the reason why such passages are not graceful in music; and first concerning the consecution of 5ths and 8ves.

These two are called Perfect Concords, not only because their sound is more perfect or more perfectly fixed than that of the other consonants which are subordinate to them, but also because they arise from the first two proportions that are found in numbers, viz. an 8ve from Dupla, and a 5th from Sesquialtera as I showed pages 52 and 53.

Now as to the disallowance of their following one another of the same kind, you may observe that our senses are still delighted with variety, as we may instance in this. Suppose an excellent dish of meat, prepared with greatest industry to please the taste, were set before us to feed on, would it not be more acceptable to have some variety after it than to have the same over again? The very same it is in sounds presented to our ear, for no man that hath skill in music can hear two perfect 5ths or two 8ves betwixt the same parts, rising or falling together, but his ear will be displeased with the latter of them because he expected in place thereof some other concord.[15]

This reason against the consecution of 5th and 8ves being admitted, we will now proceed to the other disallowances which, upon due examination, we shall find to arise from the very same consequence.

For the better understanding of this, you must know first, that every disallowance doth end either in an 8ve or in a 5th (by these I also mean their octaves). Secondly, that a disallowance is commonly generated by both the parts moving the same way. Thirdly, that every leap in music doth imply a transition by degrees from the former to the latter note by which the leap is formed. Lastly, that those implicit degrees, by reason of both parts moving the same way, do always produce a consecution of two, if not more, perfects of the same kind.

To render this more clear, we will take some of those passages not allowed in page 22, and break the leaps into degrees according to what I showed, pages 33, 34, 'Of Breaking a Note,' as you see in the following examples:

---

[15] According to Simpson's reasoning, consecutive 3rds and 6ths should also produce a displeasing effect on the ear since there is a lack of variety. In general, however, authors offer no explanation as to why consecutive 5ths and 8ves are forbidden and this attitude developed into no exceptions to the rule being tolerated. It is therefore to Simpson's credit that he attempts an explanation, even though it is not entirely satisfactory.

By this you see that if both the parts move the same way, one of them by a degree, the other by a leap, that leap (I say) being broken into degrees begets a consecution of two perfects of the same kind, and where both parts leap the same way, if you break those leaps into degrees, there will arise from those degrees three of the same perfects. And this implicit consecution of 8ves and 5ths arising from those degrees is that which renders such passages less pleasing to the ear and are thereupon named disallowances.

These which I have shown may serve for your understanding of the rest, for they are all of the same nature excepting one which Mr. Morley and others call hitting an 8ve on the face,[16] that is, when an upper part, meeting the bass upon an 8ve, doth skip up from thence into some other perfect concord, thus:

But whereas I told you and have shown that a disallowance is commonly generated by both parts moving the same way, you must know that all passages of that sort are not disallowances, for you will hardly find a disallowance where the treble removes but one degree, except that which I showed in the first instance of the late examples where the treble falls by a degree from a 6th to an 8ve, or perhaps where the bass shall make an extravagant leap (as it were on set purpose) to meet the treble in a 5th or 8ve. In any other way I do not see how a disallowance can occur whilst the treble removes but one degree, though both parts rise or fall together. But if the treble or upper part do skip whilst the bass removes but one degree the same way, you may conclude it a disallowance.[17]

[16] Morley, *op. cit.* (ed. by R. A. Harman), pp. 147, 148.
[17] Morley permits the 5ths descending to the octave, but on p. 152 of the *Introduction* (ed. by R. A. Harman) he disapproves of an octave ascending to a fifth. The top part moves by leap 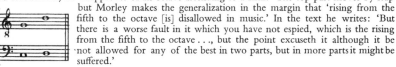 but Morley makes the generalization in the margin that 'rising from the fifth to the octave [is] disallowed in music.' In the text he writes: 'But there is a worse fault in it which you have not espied, which is the rising from the fifth to the octave . . ., but the point excuseth it although it be not allowed for any of the best in two parts, but in more parts it might be suffered.'

I will give you examples of both these ways that you may compare them by your eye and ear, and so you will better perceive what is and what is not allowed.

EXAMPLES

If you try the sound of these two ways with an instrument, you will perceive that those passages wherein the treble removes but one degree are smooth and natural, but in the other where the treble doth leap, the passage is not so pleasing to the ear.

The reason whereof (as I conceive) is because leaps are the proper movements of the bass, and degrees more natural to the treble part, as I formerly delivered in Plain Counterpoint. And therefore, so long as both parts proceed in their natural movements, the bass by leaps and the treble by degrees, the consecution is not so perceptible because it gives no offence to the ear, for that which is proper and natural cannot be displeasing. But if you disorder this natural movement by making the bass to move by a degree and the treble to leap the same way into a perfect concord, the consecution thereof presently begets a disallowance.

Lastly take notice that most of those passages we call disallowances may be tolerated in the tenor or alto, being covered by a higher part, though in the highest part itself they would not be allowable. And therefore when your treble or highest part shall make a leap, which is frequent in Figurate Descant, your chief care must be that the said treble or highest part, compared with the bass, be not guilty of any disallowance, of which there can be no danger if the leap be made into an imperfect concord.

That you may better remember them, most disallowances may be referred to these two heads:

1. When the higher part skips to a 5th or 8ve, whilst the bass removes but one degree.

2. When both parts skip the same way into a 5th or 8ve. And this is as much as I think necessary concerning disallowances.

7. CONCERNING THE CONSECUTION OF 4THS AND 5THS

I formerly showed you (page 48) three different 4ths, viz. a lesser, a greater, and a middle 4th named Diatessaron, which for distinction I call a perfect 4th because it arises from the perfect dividing of an octave into its 4th and 5th, as well [as] according to the arithmetical as the harmonical division thereof.

These 4ths are so necessary, or rather unavoidable, in composition that you shall scarcely see two, three, or more parts joined to any bass but there will frequently be one of them betwixt some two of the upper parts.

Again, three parts cannot ascend or descend together by degrees in musical concordance but there must of necessity be a consecution of so many 4ths betwixt some two of the upper parts.

Now if that consecution consist of different 4ths mixed one with another, it is very good. But if the 4ths be of the same kind, the consecution is not so allowable. The reason thereof is that 4ths are the resemblances or resonances of 5ths, as may be seen in this, that if you transpose the parts which exhibit those 4ths by placing the lower an octave higher, or setting the higher an octave lower, those 4ths will be changed into 5ths, as you may see in the following instances.

EXAMPLE

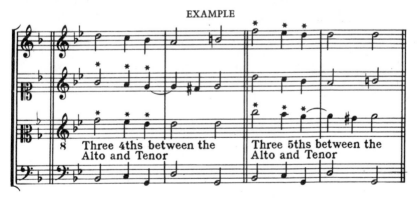

Three 4ths between the Alto and Tenor

Three 5ths between the Alto and Tenor

The notes transposed are those of the tenor in the first instance, which being placed an octave higher and so made the treble or highest part in the second instance, begets three 5ths instead of the former three 4ths.

The question now is whether these three 5ths, being of different kinds, be not allowable in composition. If they be allowed, there is less doubt to be made of the 4ths, they being also different. Here is no consecution of perfects of the same kind, for the middle 5th is imperfect. Neither is there any harshness or dissonance offered to the

ear, so near as I can perceive. And though Mr. Morley (in his Introduction, page 75)[18] with other precise composers of former times did not
allow a perfect and imperfect 5th to follow immediately one the
other, yet later authors, as well writers as composers, do both use and
approve it. See Kircher in his *Musurgia Universalis*, page 621, De li-
centia duarum Quintarum, where he cites Hieronimus Kapsperger,[19] a
very excellent author, using two 5ths one after another in divers places
of a madrigal with much art and elegancy, and in the very beginning
of the same makes no scruple of setting four 5ths, perfect and imperfect,
one after another. The example is the next which follows.

As for my own opinion, I do not only allow the consecution of
two 5ths, one of them being imperfect, but, being rightly taken, esteem
it amongst the elegances of figurate descant.

This I speak supposing them to be in short notes. But if the notes be
long, as semibreves, and sometimes also minims, I should then rather

[18] Morley, *op. cit.* (ed. by R. A. Harman), pp. 148, 149. Discussing the scholar's lesson in
counterpoint on p. 147, Morley condemns two consecutive 5ths, but owns
that 'I have seen the like committed by Master Alfonso' (Ferra- bosco,
senior, 1553–1588) and adds, 'And I myself have committed the like fault
in my first work of three parts, . . . but my fault came by negli- gence, . . .'
The editor quotes the two passages, that of Ferrabosco occurring in his five-
part madrigal, *Sich 'io cred 'ho mai*, 1587.

Morley's mistake occurs in his Canzonets for 2 and 3 Voices, No. 20, *Arise, get up.*

On p. 254 Morley mentions that Giovanni Croce, *c.* 1567–1609, 'and divers others have made
no scruple of taking those 5ths yet will we leave to imitate him in that, . . .' and goes on to
quote Zarlino: 'although we ought not to imitate them who do, without any shame, go against
the good rules and precepts of an art and a science without giving any reason for their doings. . . .'
Neither this reference to Morley nor the words of the previous two sentences —'or dissonance'
and 'they being also different' are in the second edition of the *Compendium*.

[19] Very little is known about Kapsperger. He probably died about 1640 and was a composer
of lute music, motets, etc. Kircher is unreserved in his praise for him as a composer. Simpson
refers to Kircher's work again on p. 54 of the *Compendium*.

choose to have the perfect 5th to hold on till the other part remove to a 6th before it change to an imperfect 5th.

As for example

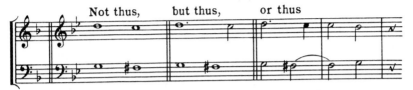

8. CONSECUTION OF 3RDS AND 6THS

Two greater 3rds can hardly follow one the other without relation inharmonical, yet in rising by degrees to a binding cadence they are allowable, as thus:

In which an inner part will properly come in, as you see in the example.

And by this you may perceive that relation inharmonical is sometimes dispensed with, which must be referred, next after the ear, to the judgement of the composer.

Two lesser 3rds may follow one another in degrees, as thus:

But in leaps they will not do so well.

Greater 6ths are answerable to lesser 3rds and therefore may follow one another, as you may see next following.

Lesser 6ths are like in nature to greater 3rds and therefore the consecution of them is liable to relation inharmonical.

Thus you have a short account [of] how 3rds and 6ths may follow one another when they are of the same kind. As for their change from greater to lesser or the contrary, it is so natural that you cannot ascend or descend either in 3rds or 6ths but it must be by a frequent changing from the lesser to the greater, or from the greater to the lesser.

Now as to their passage into other concords, the most natural is commonly that which may be done with the least remove.

Hence it is observed that the lesser 6th passes more naturally into a 5th and the greater 6th into an 8ve, as you shall see in the following instances.

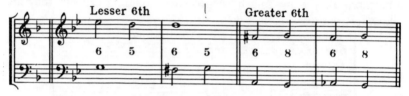

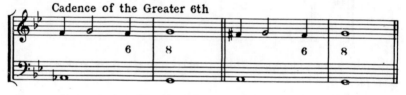

These little removes by a tone or semitone do connect or make smooth the air of the music in passing from concord to concord, which by greater removes would often seem disjointed.

I will now speak of a fugue which is the prime flower in figurate descant.

9. OF FUGA OR FUGUE[20]

This is some point (as we term it in music) consisting of 4, 5, 6, or any other number of notes, begun by some one single part and then seconded by a following part repeating the same or such like notes, sometimes in the unison or octave, but more commonly and better in a 4th or 5th above or below the leading part.

Next comes in a third part repeating the same notes, commonly in an octave or unison to the leading part.

[20] The word *fugue* used in the sense of imitation appears in Morley, *op. cit.* (ed. by R. A. Harman), p. 144. See footnote 1 on p. 80.

Then follows the fourth part, in resemblance to the second.

The fifth and sixth parts, if the composition consist of so many, do follow or come in after the same manner, one after the other, the leading parts still flying before those that follow, and from thence it hath its name fuga or fugue. The form of it you have in the following example:

Example of a fugue

Here you may observe that though the leading part begins with an even note, yet any following part may come in upon an odd note with an odd rest before it when the fugue doth require it or permit it.

Likewise take notice that you are not so strictly obliged to imitate the notes of the leading part, but that you may use a longer note instead of a shorter or the contrary when occasion shall require. Also you may rise or fall a 4th or 5th, either instead of other, which is oftentimes requisite for better maintaining the air of the music.

10. Of Arsin and Thesin[21]

Sometimes the point is inverted or moves per arsin and thesin as they phrase it; that is where the point rises in one part, it falls in another, and likewise the contrary, which produces a pleasing variety. A figure of it you may see in this instance of the former point.

An example of it you have in that which follows.

Example of a fugue per arsin and thesin

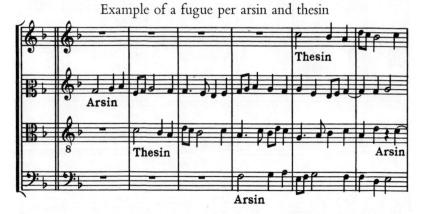

[21] The original meanings of arsis and thesis appear to have little connection with their use in the Baroque period. Both are Greek words meaning raising and lowering. In dancing the upward motion of the hand or foot was synonymous with a weak accent in poetry and downward motion with strong accent. Mediaeval times saw the use of both terms in the reverse meaning, writers then believing that the terms applied to the raising or lowering of the voice, not the hand or foot. The association of this meaning of the terms with their use in contrapuntal technique of the seventeenth and eighteenth centuries may be hazarded as arsin being the converse of thesin. The connection between the late Baroque fugue of Bach is more clearly seen in the following example by Simpson since the four entries are paired off into what might be called subject and answer.

Thus you see the point per arsin and thesin so near as I could contrive it in so short an example. Only in the 7th bar, the tenor doth not precisely express the point, which I note unto you as being [the] better of the two to injure the point than the air of the music, the design of a composer being to please the ear, rather than to satisfy the eye. Here the point was expressed both ways in each part, but it is left to your liberty whether you will have one part maintain the point per arsin, another per thesin, or what other way you shall think fit to mix them, every man being master of his own fancy.

Sometimes the point is reverted or turned backward, thus,

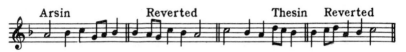

But then it must be such a point as hath no dotted note in it because the dot will stand upon the wrong side of the note when the point is reverted.

II. OF DOUBLE FUGUES[22]

Sometimes the music begins with two or more different points which the parts do interchange by turns in such manner as they did in the late inverted fugue per arsin and thesin, an example whereof you have as follows.

Example of two points moving together in fugue

[22] One of the two types of Double Fugue used in later Baroque times may stem from this use of 'Two points moving together.' It is that in which the counter-subject plays a consistent role in the structure, occurring regularly throughout the piece as an accompaniment to the subject. The double fugue which has two distinct subjects, both of which are treated in succession in two separate sections and then combined in a third section, is a second type.

By these examples you see what a fugue is. I will now lead you towards the forming thereof as children are led when they learn to go.

12. How to Form a Fugue

Having made choice of such notes as you think fit for your point, set them down in that part which you design to begin the fugue.

That done, consider which part you will have to follow next, and whether in a 4th or 5th[23] above or below the leading part. Perhaps the latter end of the fugue notes which you have set down may agree therewith. If not, you may add such other notes as may aptly meet the following part at its coming in.

Next, set down the fugue notes of that following part and add what other notes may be requisite for meeting of the third part which properly will come in upon the octave to the beginning of the leading part.

Then carry on the third part by adding such notes as may meet the beginning of the fourth part as it comes in upon an octave to the beginning of the second part. And if you rightly conceive my words and meaning, your scheme will appear like this which follows, according to the first platform of our first example of a single fugue.

---

[23] In seventeenth-century fugues the second voice frequently entered with the imitation at a distance of a 4th from the first statement. The normally accepted practise of the second voice entering with the imitation at the interval of the 5th was not consistently observed until the eighteenth century. This consistent use of the answer in the dominant key is found in Bach's fugues and he would appear to have been one of the earliest composers to adopt this procedure.

Example of the first platform of a fugue

Having done this, you may fill up the empty places with such
concords and bindings as you think fittest for carrying on your composition until you repeat the fugue in one of those parts that began it,
which may be done either in the same or in any other key that will
best maintain the air of the music, for good air is chiefly to be aimed
at in all musical composition.[24] And this repeating or renewing of the
fugue or point seems always more graceful when it comes in after some
pause or rest, by which means more notice is taken of it, as a man
that begins to speak again after some little time of silence.

The same method I have shown in four parts may also serve you
whether the parts be more or fewer.

13. Of Music composed for Voices

The ever-renowned Descartes, in the beginning of his *Compendium
of Music*, insinuates that of all sounds, the voice of man is most grateful
because it holds the greatest conformity to our spirits.[25] And (no doubt)
it is the best of music if composed and expressed in perfection.

More certain it is that of all music that ought to have the precedence
which is designed to sing and sound forth the praise and glory of the
incomprehensible Source, Soul, Essence, and Author of all created
harmony.

To this intent, masses, hymns, psalms, anthems, versicles, responsories,

---

[24] The charge Purcell laid at Simpson's door that certain passages of the book were 'destructive
to good Air which ought to be preferr'd before such Nice Rules' is to a certain extent refuted
here by this remark of Simpson's. (See Introduction, p. xxii.) It clearly shows that both Purcell
and Simpson were in complete agreement that the melodic line was of prime importance in
music, and that Simpson had no intention of making it subservient to other musical considera-
tions. It must be noted, however, that the last part of this sentence was not included in the
second edition of the *Compendium*. (See footnote 15 on p. 24.)

[25] Descartes, *A Compendium of Music*, 1650, English translation by William, Lord Brouncker,
1653, p. 1: 'This only thing seems to render the voice of Man the most gratefull of all other
sounds; that it holds the greatest conformity to our spirits.'

motets, etc., are set and sung in music, of which no man is ignorant that hath frequented either the churches beyond the sea or the cathedrals in England.

Of these forementioned, some are composed in plain counterpoint, others in figurate descant with points, fugues, syncopes, mixtures of discords, etc., according to what we have shown and taught in this present treatise.

In this divine use and application, music may challenge a preeminence above all the other mathematical sciences as being immediately employed in the highest and noblest office that can be performed by men or angels.

Neither in its civil use doth it seem inferior to any of the rest, either for art, excellency or intricacy.

Whether we consider it in its theory or mathematical part which contemplates the affections, ratios and proportions of sounds with all their nice and curious concerns.

Or in its practical part which designs, contrives and disposes those sounds into so many strange and stupendous varieties; and all from the consequence of no more than three concords and some intervening discords.

Or in its active or mechanical part which midwifes and brings forth those sounds, either by the excellent modulation of the voice, or by the exquisite dexterity of the hand upon some instrument, and thereby presents them to our ear and understanding, making such impressions upon our minds and spirits as produce those strange and admirable effects recorded in history and known by experience.

Any one of which three parts of music considered in itself is a most excellent art or science. But this is a subject might become a better orator.

Of vocal music made for the solace and civil delight of man there are many different kinds, as namely madrigals, in which fugues and all other flowers of figurate music are most frequent.

Of these you may see many sets of 3, 4, 5 and 6 parts, published both by English and Italian authors. Next the Dramatic or Recitative Music, which as yet is something a stranger to us here in England.[26] Then, Canzonets, Vilanellas, Airs of all sorts, or what else poetry hath

---

[26] It is surprising that according to Simpson, very little was known about recitative in England at this time (1667), and more surprising still that this sentence was not removed in the third edition of 1678. The introduction to Ben Johnson's masque *Vision of Delight*, 1617, was set in recitative style although Roger North, discussing Lanier's *Hero and Leander*, wrote: 'This was the first of the recitative kind that ever graced the English language, and hath bin litle followed. till the latter attempts in our theaters.' *Roger North on Music*, ed. by John Wilson, London, 1959, p. 294.

contrived to be set and sung in music. Lastly, Canons and Catches, of which we shall speak hereafter, are commonly set to words; the first, to such as be grave and serious, the latter, to words designed for mirth and recreation. Of these you may have examples sufficient in a Book of Catches sold by Mr. John Playford in the Inner Temple.

14. OF ACCOMMODATING NOTES TO WORDS

When you compose music to words, your chief endeavour must be that your notes do aptly express the sense and humour of them. If they be grave and serious, let your music be such also; if light, pleasant or lively, your music likewise must be suitable to them. Any passion of love, sorrow, anguish and the like is aptly expressed by chromatic notes and bindings. Anger, courage, revenge, etc., require a more strenuous and stirring movement. Cruel, bitter, harsh, may be expressed with a discord which, nevertheless, must be brought off according to the rules of composition. High, above, Heaven, ascend, as likewise their contraries, low, deep, down, Hell, descend, may be expressed by the example of the hand which points upward when we speak of the one and downward when we mention the other, the contrary to which would be absurd.

You must also have a respect to the points of your ditty, not using any remarkable pause or rest until the words come to a full point or period. Neither may any rest, how short soever, be interposed in the middle of a word, but a sigh or sob is properly intimated by a crotchet- or quaver-rest.

Lastly, you ought not to apply several notes nor indeed any long note to a short syllable, nor a short note to a syllable that is long. Neither do I fancy the setting of many notes to any one syllable, though much in fashion in former times, but I would have your music to be such that the words may be plainly understood.

15. OF MUSIC DESIGNED FOR INSTRUMENTS

We must now speak a little more of music made for instruments, in which points, fugues and all other figures of descant are in no less (if not in more) use than in vocal music.

Of this kind, the chief and most excellent for art and contrivance are fancies of 6, 5, 4 and 3 parts, intended commonly for viols. In this sort of music the composer, being not limited to words, doth employ all his art and invention solely about the bringing in and carrying on of these fugues according to the order and method formerly shown.

When he has tried all the several ways which he thinks fit to be used therein, he takes some other point and does the like with it, or else for variety, introduces some chromatic notes with bindings and inter-mixtures of discords, or falls into some lighter humour like a madrigal or what else his own fancy shall lead him to, but still concluding with something which hath art and excellency in it.

Of this sort you may see many compositions made heretofore in England by Alfonso Ferabosco, Coperario, Lupo, White, Ward, Mico, Dr. Colman, and many more now deceased. Also by Mr. Jenkins, Mr. Locke, and divers other excellent men, doctors and bachelors in music yet living.[27]

This kind of music (the more is the pity) is now much neglected by reason of the scarcity of auditors that understand it, their ears being better acquainted and more delighted with light and airy music.

The next in dignity[28] after a fancy is a pavan which some derive from Padua in Italy, at first ordained for a grave and stately manner of dancing (as most instrumental musics were in their several kinds, fancies and symphonies excepted) but now grown up to a height of composition made only to delight the ear.

A pavan, be it of 2, 3, 4, 5 or 6 parts, doth commonly consist of three strains, each strain to be played twice over. Now as to any piece of music that consists of strains, take these following observations.

All music concludes in the key of his composition which is known by the bass as hath been shown. This key hath always other keys proper to it for middle closes (see pages 23, 24). If your pavan, or what else, be of three strains, the first strain may end in the key of the composition as the last doth, but the middle strain must always end in the key of a middle close.

Sometimes the first strain does end in a middle close and then the middle strain must end in some other middle close, for two strains following immediately one another ought not to end in the same key. The reason thereof is obvious; to wit, the ending still in the same key doth reiterate the air too much and different endings produce more variety.[29] Therefore when there are but two strains, let the first end in a middle close, that both strains may not end alike.

---

[27] Alfonso Ferabosco, c. 1575–1628. Giovanni Coperario, c. 1570(?)–1626. Thomas Lupo—two members of the same family both have this name, either or both of them being responsible for about eighty viol fantasies; one of them died in 1628, the other before 1660. Mathew White, ?–?, sixteenth–seventeenth-century composer. John Ward, ?–?, sixteenth–seventeenth-century composer. Richard Mico, ?–?, died before 1667. Dr. Charles Coleman, ?–?, died before July 9th, 1664. John Jenkins, 1592–1678. Mathew Locke, c. 1630–1677.

All these composers are the subjects of articles in Grove's *Dictionary*, fifth edition, 1954.

[28] = in importance.

[29] This sentence first appeared in the 3rd edition of the *Compendium*.

I do confess I have been guilty myself of this particular fault (by the example of others) in some things which I composed long since, but I willingly acknowledge my error that others may avoid it.

Next in course after a pavan follows a galliard, consisting sometimes of two and sometimes of three strains. Concerning their endings, I refer you to what was last said of a pavan. This, according to its name, is of a lofty and frolic movement. The measure of it, always a tripla of three minims to a time.

An allemande, so called from the country whence it came, as the former from Gallia, is always set in common time like a pavan but of a quicker and more airy movement. It commonly hath but two strains and therefore the first ought to end in a middle key.

In these and other airy musics of strains which now pass under the common name of airs, you will often hear some touches of points or fugues, but not insisted upon or continued as in fancy-music.

I need not enlarge my discourse to things so common in each ones ears as courantes, sarabandes, jigs, country dances, etc.,[30] of which sorts I have known some who by a natural aptness and accustomed hearing of them would make suchlike, being untaught, though they had not so much skill in music as to set them down in notes.

Seeing this Compendium cannot contain examples of all these which I give you account of, I would advise you to procure some of such kinds as you most affect and set them down in score, one part under another as the examples are set in this book, that they may serve you as a pattern to imitate.

But let them be of some of the best esteemed composers in that kind of music.

You need not seek outlandish authors, especially for instrumental music, no nation in my opinion being equal to the English in that way, as well for their excellent, as their various and numerous Consorts of 3, 4, 5 and 6 parts, made properly for instruments, of all which, as I said, fancies are the chief.

[30] The original spelling of the names of these dances has been altered. Simpson's spelling was as follows: Galiard, Almane, Corants, Sarabands, Jiggs.

THE FIFTH PART

TEACHING THE CONTRIVANCE OF CANON

1. Concerning Canon

A CANON is a fugue,[1] so bound up or restrained that the following part or parts must precisely repeat the same notes with the same degrees rising or falling which were expressed by the leading part, and because it is tied to so strict a rule, it is thereupon called a canon.

Divers of our countrymen have been excellent in this kind of music, but none that I meet with have published any instructions for making a canon.

Mr. Elway Bevin professes fair in the title page of his book and gives us many examples of excellent and intricate canons of divers sorts, but not one word of instruction how to make suchlike.

Mr. Morley in his *Introduction to Music*, page 172, says thus:

A canon may be made in any distance comprehended within the reach of the voice, as the third, fifth, sixth, seventh, eighth, ninth, tenth, eleventh, twelfth, or other, but for the composition of canons, no general rule can be given as that which is performed by plain sight, wherefore I will refer it to your own study to find out such points as you shall think meetest to be followed and to frame and make them fit for your canon.[2]

If, as Mr. Morley says, no general rule can be given, our business must be to try what helps we can afford a learner towards the making of a canon. I am the more inclined to offer unto you this little essay upon it because the exercise thereof will much enable you in all other kinds of composition, especially where anything of fugue is concerned, of which it is the principal. And I will direct you in the same method which I did before in contriving a single fugue, that is, first to set down your material notes and then to accommodate your other descant to those notes.

---

[1] See footnote 20 on p. 70. Morley uses the term fugue to mean canon. Morley, *op. cit.* (ed. by R. A. Harman), p. 180. The word fuga which is the Italian for fugue (as well as the Latin for flight) was used originally to mean canon by mediaeval and renaissance composers. Only in the seventeenth century did fuga assume the meaning of pieces constructed from imitative entries.

[2] Morley, *op. cit.* (ed. by R. A. Harman), p. 283. In a footnote, the editor points out that, 'It is odd that the fourth is omitted, as M. gives a rule for composing one on pp. 180 and 182.' On p. 180 Morley's view as expressed in Simpson's text is to be found again. In answer to a question of Philomathes, 'What, be there no rules to be observed in the making of two parts in one upon a plainsong?' the Master replies 'No, verily, in that the form of making the canons is so many and divers ways altered that no general rule may be gathered; . . .'

2. CANON OF TWO PARTS

We will, for more ease, begin with two parts and I will take the first two semibreves of a former fugue to let you see the way and manner of it. The canon shall be set in a 5th above and then your first notes will stand thus:

By 5th, 6th, 7th, etc., above or below is understood the distance of the key betwixt the beginning notes of either part.

Having set down your beginning notes, your next business is to fill up that vacant space in the second bar with what descant you please, which may be done in this manner.

Now seeing that the following part must also sing the same notes in a 5th above, it necessarily follows that you must transfer the said new notes to the upper part and apply new descant to them also, and in this manner you are to proceed from bar to bar, still applying new descant to the last removed notes.

In this manner you may continue two parts in one to what length you please. A short example may suffice to let you see the way of it.

EXAMPLE

Take notice that the canon ends where you see the little arches over either part.[3] The rest is only to make up the conclusion as we commonly do, unless we design the parts to begin over again and so to go round without a conclusion.

In the foregoing example, the following part came in above the other part. We will now take a view of it coming in under the leading

[3] See footnote 21 on p. 13.

part and after a semibreve rest. The method is the same, only in this we must remove the new added descant downward as before we carried it upward, still making new descant to the last removed notes.

EXAMPLE

Whether your following part comes in after a semibreve or minim rest, more or less, the method is the same, as you may see in this next following in which the lower part comes in after a minim rest.

EXAMPLE

Neither is there any more difficulty in setting your canon a 7th, 9th, or any other distance either above or below than in these which I have already shown, as you may see by the next following set in a 9th above.

EXAMPLE

This, I suppose, is sufficient to let you see with how much ease, being a little exercised in it, two parts in one may be carried on to what length or shortness you please.

3. CANON OF THREE PARTS

We will now make trial of three parts in one, carried on by the same method, in which the notes of the leading part must be removed upward or downward according as the following parts come in, either above or below the leading part.

I will first set down the beginning notes of each part as I formerly did of a single fugue that you may see the first platform thereof, thus:

That being done, the first business is to fill up the second bar of the leading part with some note or notes which may agree with that
• part which came in next after it and add the said note or notes to each of the other parts in this manner.

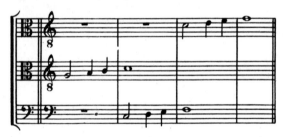

Then fill up the third bar of the leading part with some note or notes which may agree with both the other parts, still adding the said note or notes to the other parts, and thus you are to do from bar to bar.

But if you perceive that your following parts begin to run counter one upon another by these additional notes, you must then try some other way, either by putting in a rest, or by altering the course or notes of the leading part, and in this particular it is (as Mr. Morley said) that canon is performed by plain sight.

Example of three parts in one

If you would have your canon to go round, the conclusion must
be omitted and each part must begin again when it comes to that note
which is marked with a little arch over it where the canon ends. And
the rests which are set at the beginning, before the following parts,
must be left out, and then the usual way of writing it down is only the
leading part set alone with marks directing where the other parts come
in, as follows:

A3 Canon in the fifth below and fourth above

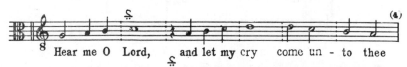

Hear me O Lord,   and let my cry   come un - to thee

4. OF CANON IN UNISON

The same method might serve for a canon in unison, that is to say,
the leading part must be accommodated to the following part when
it comes in and to both parts when they sound together.

But I will give you a nearer notion of it. In reference whereto you
may consider that seeing each part doth begin in the same tone, it

---

[4] The places where the two other voices enter are marked by the use of the sign   (see p. 13)
which occurs above the stave in the second bar and below the stave in the third bar.
This is misleading as it would seem to indicate that the voice a fourth above enters a bar before
the voice a fifth below, which is not the case as the written-out example of three parts in one
shows. Another method of notating a canon appears on p. 91.

necessarily follows that the foregoing parts must move into the concords of the said tone, either ascending or descending, and by this means the sound of the same tone will be continued so long as the parts move in the concords of that key.

As for example,

By this you see what concords your canon must move into, your care being no more than to avoid the consecution of perfects of the same kind and to dispose your parts so much as you can into different concords.

Example of canon in unison

5. Of Syncopated or Driving Canon

There is another sort of canon in unison in which the following parts come in upon a crotchet or upon a minim rest one after another, and this kind of canon may be applied to any ground or plainsong consisting of semibreves or of breves if you double the length of the descant notes.

I will first show the way of it upon semibreves moving by degrees.

EXAMPLE

The figures show the concords of the leading part to the ground both ascending and descending. If the ground consist of breves, the length of the descant notes must be doubled. And this, I think, may suffice to let you see the order of your descant in those places where the ground of plainsong shall rise or fall by degrees.

I will now let you see how to order your descant when the ground shall move by leaps.

In which the movement of your descant must be from 3rd to 3rd and your leading part must also meet each note of the ground in a 3rd, both which are easily effected as you may see by the following instances.

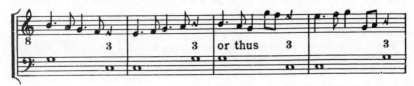

Also you have liberty to break a minim into two crotchets and to set one of them in an octave above or below when there shall be occasion for it.

You shall now see the former degrees and these leaps mixed one with another in this following example.

A4 Canon in unison to a ground

Here you see the leading part still beginning upon a 3rd to each note of the ground, also a 6th and 5th following after the 3rd to meet the next note of the bass when it rises[5] one degree, according to what was shown in the example of degrees.

I will now set down this canon in plain notes that you may better perceive both the syncopation and also how the parts move from 3rd to 3rd,[6] excepting where the bass removes but one degree, in which places they make a leap to a 4th. Also you may observe in the leading part, and likewise those that follow, two places where a minim is

---

[5] The word 'it' refers to the leading part.
[6] These intervals are not measured from the bass; they are the distances of the notes of the melodic line as d', f', a', d'', = 3rd, 3rd, 3rd, 4th.

broken into two crotchets and one of them set an octave lower for better carrying on the air of the descant and keeping the parts within due compass.

EXAMPLE

We will try one example more in this way upon longer notes of the ground, the descant notes being made proportionate thereto.

A4 canon in unison upon breves

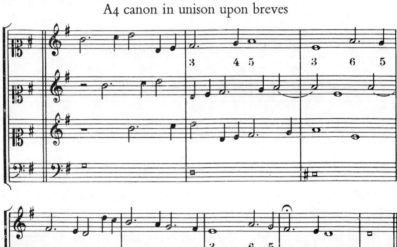

In these syncopated canons you may observe that two of the parts do move up and down in an even measure and the other part, by reason of its coming in upon an odd rest, doth drive or break in betwixt them.

After the same manner of syncopation or driving, canons may be made, though not upon a ground, the parts being set a 4th, 5th or 8ve one from another, as you may see by these two following, made by the excellent Mr. Matthew Locke.[7]

A3 canon in the 8ve and 4th below

A3 canon in the 5th below and 4th above

The rule or method of which is this, that the parts, whether ascending or descending, proceed from 3rd to 3rd like the former two canons in unison and break off to a 4th the contrary way to keep the canon in due decorum, which otherwise would ascend or descend beyond due limits.

The position of the parts is according to the harmonical division of an octave which hath its 5th in the lower place. The driving part is the sub-octave, as you may perceive in their examples.

[7] The phrase, *Composer in Ordinary to His Majesty*, was added after the name, Mr. Mathew Locke, in the third edition, but this title was given after his name in his letter of recommendation in the second edition of the Compendium. Simpson spells the name, Lock. Locke was probably created Composer in Ordinary to His Majesty for the music which he composed to be performed during the Royal Procession from the Tower to Whitehall on the day before the coronation of Charles II, 22nd April, 1661. The acknowledgment of Simpson's debt to Locke (see Part V, Chapter 6) first appeared in the 3rd edition of the *Compendium*.

6. OF CANON A NOTE HIGHER OR LOWER

Canon a note higher is when each part comes in a tone or note above another, as you may see in this next following, made by the forenamed Mr. Locke, to whom I do acknowledge myself much obliged both for his suggestions and assistance in this treatise. This depends upon sight and therefore no rule to be given excepting the helps formerly mentioned.

Canon a note higher

Canon a note lower is when the parts come in a tone or note under each other, as you may see by the next following, made by our first proposed method with some little reference to sight.

EXAMPLE

Which may be written in one single part and marked in manner as follows:

A3 canon a note lower

Where note that the following parts come in as they stand in backward order behind the leading part. And this is the best way of marking a canon, especially when the following parts come in upon several keys which may be known by the several clefs which denote those keys and do also show the compass of the canon.

7. OF CANON RISING OR FALLING A NOTE

There is another sort of canon which rises or falls a note each time it is repeated and may be composed by our first method, only you must contrive it so that it may end aptly for that purpose.

EXAMPLE

Canon rising a note each repetition

Canon falling a note each repetition

8. OF RETROGRADE CANON OR CANON RECTE AND RETRO

Some canons are made to be sung Recte and Retro, as they phrase it, that is forward and backward, or one part forward and another backward, which may seem a great mystery and a business of much intricacy before one knows the way of doing it. But that being known,

---

[8] A similar method of notating a canon is given in the *Compendium* on p. 84. See footnote 4 on p. 84.

[9] The so-called spiral canon. The first four bars are repeated six times so that the music passes through the keys on the notes of the whole tone scale, G major, F major, E ♭ major, D ♭ major, etc.

it is the easiest of all sorts of canons. This which follows shall serve for an example of it.

Canon Recte and Retro

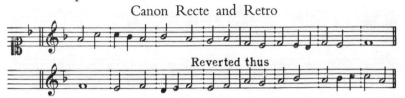

Either of these alone is a canon of two parts, one part singing forward, the other beginning at the wrong end and singing the notes backward. The composition whereof is no more than this which follows.

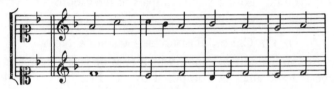

Only the end of one part is joined to the end of the other in a retrograde form as upon examination you will easily find if you look back upon the stroke which you see drawn through the middle of either. And after the same manner you may add more parts to them if you please.

There is another way of composing music to be played or sung forward and backward (much to the same effect) which is by making the parts double, as two trebles, two basses, etc., as you see here following.

EXAMPLE

Here you have two trebles and two basses which as they now stand may be played or sung as well backward as forward and will resemble a lesson[10] of two strains, the first forward and the second strain backward as upon trial you will perceive. But if you would have one part to be sung backward whilst the other sings forward, you must then turn one of the trebles and likewise one of the basses the contrary way and join them together so that their two ends may meet in the middle of the lesson, as you see in the following example, and then the harmony will be right whether you sing them backward or forward, or one part forward and the other part backward. Likewise two may sing the treble, one forward, the other backward, and [the] other two, the bass in like manner and then it is a canon of four parts in two.

EXAMPLE

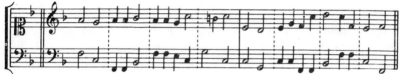

In like manner you may compose six parts in three, or eight parts in four by adding two altos or two tenors or both and then joining their ends together as we did these trebles and basses.

By this which hath been shown, I suppose you see the way of Retrograde Descant. But I must advise[11] you not to set any notes with dots after them in this way of Recte and Retro because the dots in the Retro will stand on the wrong side of the notes. Also you must be wary how you use discords therein lest in the revert or Retro they hit upon the beginning instead of the latter part of the note.

9. OF DOUBLE DESCANT

It is called double descant when the parts are so contrived that the treble may be made the bass and the bass the treble. I will give you an example of it in canon and per arsin and thesin that, for brevity, I may comprise both under one, as in the example next following.

Double Descant in Canon per Arsin and Thesin

[10] The word _lesson_ is the seventeenth-century equivalent of the modern word _piece_.
[11] Simpson writes: 'But I must advertise you.' See footnote 17 on p. 25.

This may seem a difficult business to one that is not very ready in his sight but I shall render it as plain and easy as I did the first examples of two parts in one, for it may be performed by the same method. Only in this, you must invert the notes as you place them in the following part, accommodating your new descant, bar after bar, to the notes so inverted, as you may easily perceive by this instance of its beginning.

But I must give you one caveat,[12] which is that you must not use any 5ths in this kind of double descant unless in passage or binding like a discord, because when you change the parts, making that the treble which before was the bass (which is called the Reply) those 5ths will be changed into 4ths.

The Reply

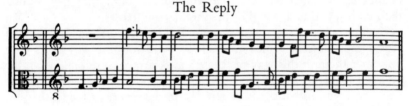

The canon began in unison which in the reply is changed into an 8ve, but the same method serves in what distance soever it be set.

10. OF CANON TO A PLAINSONG PROPOSED

I showed you formerly how to compose a canon in unison to any ground or plainsong consisting of semibreves or breves and gave you rules for it. But this which I am now to speak of cannot be reduced to any rule that I know as depending merely upon sight, and therefore all we can do is only to give you what help or assistance we are able towards the effecting of it.

We will take, for instance, one of Mr. Elway Bevin's, not to be named without due praise for his excellent book of canons, printed 1631,[13] where you have examples of canons upon the same plainsong in all the distances contained in an octave, of which this is one.

---

[12] = law or rule.   [13] See Introduction, p. xxxiii.

Now as to the contrivance. First you are to consider what notes will serve your present purpose for the leading part and also suit your following part in reference to the next note of the plainsong. When you have found out notes that will fit both these occasions, set them down and then your beginning will stand in this manner.

Then you are to fill up the vacant bar of the leading part with such notes as may also serve the following part in reference to the next succeeding note of the plainsong, thus:

And in this manner you are to proceed from bar to bar, still filling the empty bar of the leading part with such notes as may agree both with the present note of the plainsong and serve the following part for the next note of the plainsong also.

The same method is to be observed though the plainsong be placed betwixt or above the other parts. As also, whether your canon be set in a 4th, 6th, 7th, 9th or any other distance either above or below, as you may see by these two following examples.

Canon in the 13th below

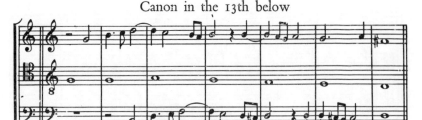

Canon in the 9th above

11. Of Catch or Round[14]

I must not omit another sort of canon in more request and common use (though of less dignity) than all those which we have mentioned, and that is a Catch or Round. Some call it a canon in unison or a canon consisting of periods. The contrivance whereof is not intricate, for if you compose any short strain of three or four parts, setting them all within the ordinary compass of a voice and then place one part at the end of another in what order you please so as they may aptly make one continued tune, you have finished a Catch.

EXAMPLE

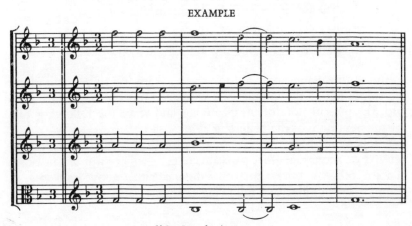

[14] See Introduction, p. xxx.

Here you have the parts as they are composed, and next you shall have them set one at the end of another, with a mark directing where the following parts are to come in, as you see in this following example.

A Catch of four parts

Having given you these lights and instructions for the contrivance of canon, which is the last and esteemed the intricatest part of composition, I must refer the exercise of it to your own study and industry.

And now I have delivered, though in brief, all such instructions as I thought chiefly necessary for your learning of practical music. But it rests on your part to put them in practice, without which nothing can be effected. For by singing a man is made a singer, and by composing he becomes a composer. 'Tis practice that brings experience, and experience begets that knowledge which improves all arts and sciences.

FINIS

APPENDIX

SHORT AND EASY

AYRES

DESIGNED

FOR LEARNERS

100

¹ Simpson gives the sign $\stackrel{S}{\div}$ here.
² These notes are written as dotted breves in the original.

³ These notes are written as two tied minims in the original.

4 Simpson gives the sign $\frac{S}{\div}$ here.

13

14

⁵ Simpson gives the sign ⨣ here.

106

For two Bass-Viols

[6] In the third edition the bass-viol parts were printed seperately on opposite pages of the opened book. The second bass-viol part was printed upside down so that two instrumentalists could face each other with the book between them and so perform the piece.

[7] Written as a breve rest in the third edition.

[8] E in the original.

[9] Repeat indicated in the second part only.

10 B♭ in the original.

4

(11)

11 B♭ in the original.

5

¹²The rhythm of the second part in the third edition is given as | ♩ ♪♪. ♪|

6

13 This piece is written in that notation described by Simpson on p.16 using
blackened semibreves and minims.

For Sir John St. Barbe, Baronet

14 The top part was originally written in that tablature described by Simpson on p.4   The bass part was written in staff notation. These pieces were written to be played with or without the bass part.

15 Written as two quavers in the third edition.

16 The repeat sign :∥: occurs both in the middle and at the end of this piece. Both parts are therefore to be repeated.

112

¹⁷Written as F in the third edition.

THE END   J[ohn] B[olles?]

Lessons by Sundry Authors for the Treble Bass-Viol, and Harp.

[18] This sharp is misplaced and written before the A in the third edition.

[19] Both repeat signs :[|: and $\frac{S}{\cdot\cdot}$ occur here. Both parts are therefore to be repeated.

[20] C is sharpened in the third edition, but no accidental is prefixed before the following B. The sharp has therefore been omitted in the present edition.

[21] These numbered pieces are notated in the same way as those for two bass-viols (see footnote 6 on p. 106

First and second time bars are shown in this manner:-

Francis Forcer

116

3 Two Parts

4

Francis Forcer

1 Two Parts

118

3 Two Parts

24 In the third edition, D in the treble and B in the bass have pause marks over them. The return to the first strain is not indicated in the original.

(26)Francis Forcer

FINIS

25 B in the treble is written as a quaver in the third edition.

26 The name of Francis Forcer (c. 1650-1750) is to be found at the bottom of those pages on which the numbered lessons are printed. Forcer was for a time (c. 1697) the joint holder of the lease of the Wells and the Music-house. Some of his compositions were published by Playford in *Choice Ayres and Dialogues*, 1679, but many are still in manuscript and preserved in the Fitzwilliam Library, the British Museum, and the Library of Christ Church College, Oxford.

27 This lesson, unlike the previous numbered ones, is written with the parts under each other in score.